Buddhism Beginners Guide

Buddha's Teaching From the Dalai Lama

BUDDHISM BEGINNERS GUIDE: BUDDHA'S TEACHING
FROM THE DALAI LAMA

TABLE OF CONTENTS

Introduction 8

Chapter 1: The Man Behind Buddhism .. 11

    What is Buddhism? 11

    A Look at the Life of Siddhartha Gautama 15

    The Fragmentation of Buddhism and the Different Schools 25

Chapter 2: A General Look at the Teachings of Buddha 35

    The Chain of Causation 36

    The Noble Eightfold Path 39

    The Three Fires of Buddhism 41

Chapter 3: The Foundation of Buddhism - The Four Noble Truths 43

    The Truth of Suffering *(Dukkha)* 46

    The Truth of Cessation *(Nirodha)* 54

    The Truth of the Path *(Magga)* 55

Chapter 4: Walking the Noble Eightfold Path 58

    Right Understanding 59

    Right Thought 59

    Right Speech 59

    Right Action 60

Right Livelihood 60
Right Effort 60
Right Mindfulness 61
Right Concentration 61

Chapter 5: Suffering, Karma, Nirvana and Reincarnation According to Buddhism. 64

What is Suffering in Buddhism 64
What Does Nirvana Stand For in Buddhism?
.... 69
Understanding Karma 73
A Piece on Reincarnation 79

Chapter 6: The Current State of Buddhism
.... 91

Using Buddhism as a Moral Compass 92
Embracing Buddhism as a Lifestyle 93

Chapter 7: The Core Practices of Buddhism 98

Mindfulness Meditation 98
Chanting and Mantras 100
Vegetarian or Vegan Lifestyle 101

Chapter 8: Learning to Practice the Five Precepts of Buddhism 103

Why is it Important to Follow Precepts? 103
The Five Precepts Broken Down 104
The Overall Meaning of the Five Precepts .. 109

Chapter 9: Understand the Soul of Light and Enlightenment 112

    Aid Others 113

    Practicing the Divine Abodes 113

    The Six Perfections 115

Chapter 10: Exploring the Treasures and Poisons of Buddhism 125

    The Buddha.. 125

    The Dharma 126

    The Sangha... 127

    Moha or Delusion 128

    Raga or Greed 128

    Dvesha or Ill Will 129

Chapter 11: The Art of Practicing Buddhism in Day-to-Day Life 132

    The Benefits of Practicing Buddhism in Everyday Life 132

    Practicing Buddhism 135

    Setting Up Your Homespace For Meditation 140

Chapter 12: Understanding How Yoga can Bring Peace to Your Mind 151

    Where Does Yoga Originate From? 151

    What Exactly is Yoga?............................. 153

    The Different Schools of Yoga 155

The Practices of a Yogi 157

The Health Benefits of Yoga 160

Chapter 13: Using Meditation as a Weapon Against Stress and Anxiety 178

How Can Meditation Help With Anxiety and Depression 178

How Can Meditation Help With Relationship Anxiety 190

What Exactly is Meditation? 200

How Does Meditation Work? 202

Why Should You Practice Meditation? 206

The Impacts of Meditation on Your Daily Life 208

Chapter 14: Getting Rid of Your Negative Thoughts 219

What is Self -Talk? 219

The Four Main Categories of Negative Self-Talk 227

How to Overcome Personalization .. 258

Chapter 15: Letting Go of Anger 266

How Do You Define Anger? 266

Looking at the common triggers of anger ... 275

The Benefits Of Letting Go Of Anger 277

Learning to Identify the Causes of Anger ... 280

The Importance of Breaking the Cycle of Hatred 282

Deal With Your Emotional Burden and Let Go of Destructive Habits 300

Mental Exercises to Keep Yourself Calm.....335

Chapter 16: The Minimalistic Life - Baby Steps to Buddhism 339

Chapter 17: The Different Rituals of Buddhism to Know About 345

Bowing Down to Show Respect 346

The Different Chants 347

Importance Of Gongs 347

Incense Lighting 348

Altar Offerings 349

Taking Shelter/Refuge................................349

Confessing Your Sins 350

Precept Ceremony......................................352

Dedication of Merit....................................353

Embracing The Art Of Meditation...............353

Chapter 18: What to do Next? 356

Take Regular Walks of Contemplation........356

Try to Make Friends With a Spiritual Side.. 357

Explore Buddhist Musicians........................ 357

Use Mindfulness Apps 358

We can practice mindfulness and meditation on the go, thanks to mobile technology. So, if you're having difficulty finding time to explore your religion, apps can be extremely helpful. Several smartphone applications allow us to practice meditation at times of the day when we are least likely to do so: 358

Conclusion 360

Introduction

Most people don't know this, but despite being a concept that is pretty much thousands of years old, Buddhism is now more popular than it ever was.

You can seamlessly tell this by the influx of so many books based on explaining Buddhism's concepts and the number of monks you see on the street, not to mention the rise of yoga and Buddhist schools all across the globe!

People from all different sectors of life, from common citizens to famous movie stars, have slowly begun to incorporate various practices of Buddhism, such as yoga and meditation into their lifestyle to stay healthy and psychologically sound, and the numbers just keep growing by the day.

But despite its rising popularity, there are still thousands of people out there who are completely unaware of what exactly "Buddhism" really is and what it entails.

Ask anyone, and most people will tell you that Buddhism is a form of religion, but this is as far away from the truth as it can get! Buddhism is not a religion; it is more of a way of life that is very meticulously designed to give you mental peace in a world where everything else seems to just bring you nothing but frustration.

People with little knowledge will tell you that people who follow Buddhism imprison themselves into a life full of rules that goes to the extremes and that they don't have any joy left in their life. But that's the point where they are completely wrong!

Buddhism doesn't enforce anything upon you. If you want to be a monk and leave all the earthly pleasures for the sake of nirvana, you can do it on your own accord. If you want to be a Christian and just follow Buddhism's rituals and norms to bring a sense of peace in your life, you can do it too!

Buddhism is not created to keep you under pressure; rather, it was conceived to help you break free from all the anxiety and stress of this world and lead a happier and blissful life.

Suppose you are a complete beginner and have just started exploring out the concepts of Buddhism. In that case, chances are that everything is feeling a bit complex and convoluting to you, and that is quite normal, as Buddhism is a rather complex topic to deal with. Still, it doesn't have to be that way, now does it?

The primary focus is to help you understand Buddhism's ins and outs and guide you into building a very strong foundation which you can start incorporating the practices of Buddhism into your current lifestyle.

While writing this book, my goal was to ensure that even the absolute beginners can pick it up and learn more about the subject matter with ease.

All of the information is divided into their own chapters, further broken down into sub-sections that will help you read through the book at your own leisurely pace.

Throughout the book, I will walk you through the very root of Buddhism and help you understand how Buddhism was conceived in the first place. I will also introduce you to the Dalai Lama and help you familiarize yourself with the teachings of Buddhism, the Noble Eightfold Path, the Four Noble Truths, the Five Precepts of Buddhism and much more.

In short, this is the only book that you are ever going to want to read if you need the most perfect entry point into the world of Buddhism.

So, what are you waiting for? Go ahead and start exploring!

BUDDHISM BEGINNERS GUIDE: BUDDHA'S TEACHING
FROM THE DALAI LAMA

Chapter 1: The Man Behind Buddhism

What is Buddhism?

Contrary to popular belief, Buddhism is not a religion. It is not in the strictest terms where people are expected to believe in the faith. Many people make the error and avoid Buddhism because they think it contradicts their church's teachings. However, you can practice Buddhism alongside, or in addition, to your personal beliefs and religion.

There is no god to worship, although you might wonder why some people seem to worship Buddha statues. Although some worship his portrait (incorrectly), real Buddhists merely pay reverence to the Buddha's memory. They do not worship or pray to him. The Buddha himself serves as a guide and instructor for those seeking enlightenment. The altars found in Buddhist temples are inspirational and serve to remind

Buddhists of the direction they have chosen to travel. The colors of a Buddhist temple's decoration are made up of colors easily seen by the eye, and the Buddha statue serves as a guide to your meditative phase.

The gentle image of the Buddha inspires many people who wake up each morning to follow Buddhist teachings. It's similar to getting inspiration from the words of a good individual. When life becomes overwhelming, and your mind starts to wander, his calm and meditative image will help you understand and remember the following teachings. As a result, building a meditative space and decorating it with a Buddha statue or other inspiring objects is popular among westerners.

Buddhism is a way of life that leads to the realization of true truth. Its teachings focus on improving your ability to be aware of your emotions, behavior, and surroundings. All of this leads to a life in harmony with nature and your true self. You may find it difficult to comprehend at first. Still, all that occurs in your life is determined by your emotions. When you meditate, you get a better picture of what needs to improve in your world and understand more about who you are about the world that you reside in, or even the body you occupy.

Buddhism's practices, such as meditation and yoga, are intended to help you unlearn your preconceived notions about yourself and the world. They serve as a reference for you to embrace virtues, such as goodness, compassion, true wisdom, and sensitivity. We are taught society values in our childhood, which may or may not be consistent with true values, so this reminder is essential. Look at the world's confusion, and you can still find a line of thinking that leads you to the unhappiness you are experiencing. This could be a prejudice against certain members of society, or it could be a sense of self-worth caused by your interactions with society.

Those who continue to walk the Buddhist path normally achieve the state of "perfect enlightenment." In other words, they turn into a "Buddha." A Buddha is a being who has been able to see the true essence of creation. The enlightened being then proceeds to live life to the fullest, adhering to the values consistent with this vision. Since this theory will call into question your current motivation, values, and way of life, you must be open-minded enough to learn because the teachings are extensive. To achieve enlightenment, you must be able to let go of ideas that might be central to who you are at the moment.

The idea of enlightenment can be broken down into two simple forms - the mind and the self. The mind is that constant voice that has been molded and constructed based on the world around you in this life. Self is that inner being separate from your body's meat and does not change based on any teachings or experiences that life brings you. Your real self is what can be understood to travel from life to life during reincarnation.

In different belief systems, these are given names, such as the soul, although what name you give it isn't important. It is merely important that you recognize that these two parts of you exist and that, if you are unhappy in your life, harmony or balance is missing. That's where Buddhism helps you align these values so that both parts of you are in harmony with each other.

Each and every living being has the opportunity to become enlightened in each life they live. There is no set course or prewritten script for your life. As discussed later in this book, Karma plays a part in deciding the circumstances in which you will be born into from life to life, but your own spiritual and mental ambition are what drives each person to take one step closer to full enlightenment.

However, things get interesting here because when you follow Buddhism's path, you do not have an "end goal." It is a paradox for one to declare that they are going to practice Buddhism to reach enlightenment.

A Look at the Life of Siddhartha Gautama

Siddhartha Gautama was born in the Himalayan foothills around 567 BCE into the Shakya clan, of which his father was the chief. According to legend, when Siddhartha Gautama was about 12 years old, the Brahmins — members of the highest Hindu class who were priests, teachers, and overall protectors of sacred learning — prophesied that he would either be a collective monarch or a celebrated holy man. His father confined him inside the palace walls, where Siddhartha Gautama grew up in luxury. He was imprisoned within the castle walls to keep him from becoming a holy man, also known as an ascetic. An ascetic is someone who practices intense self-denial and lives a simple life while following spiritual goals. This was not the life his father desired for him, so he protected him from the outside world in the expectation that Siddhartha Gautama would develop into a great ruler.

Siddhartha Gautama was taught to swim and wrestle, as well as archery and swordsmanship. Siddhartha Gautama eventually married his cousin Yagodhara, and they had a son called Rahula. It was normal for royal families to marry among themselves because no-one else was considered equal to them; they wanted to keep the royal line pure. Siddhartha Gautama's life was complete and rich; in today's world, he would be one of those people who have it all: money, luxury, a wife, and a boy. With all of this happiness and comfort, what could possibly be the cause of Siddhartha Gautama's dissatisfaction?

Siddhartha Gautama had a longing, a desire to know more, and a disappointment with his life. This yearning drove him to venture beyond the palace walls. He came across three things in Kapilavastu: an elderly man, a sick man, and a dead body being taken to the grounds for burning. Siddhartha Gautama had never seen such things in his sheltered life — he was unprepared; he had no idea what was going on in front of him. His chariot driver explained it to him simply: any living being ages, becomes ill, and finally dies. This knowledge filled Siddhartha Gautama with dread and apprehension.

He saw an ascetic wearing a robe on his way back to the palace and carrying a sadhu, or holy man's mug. Siddhartha Gautama then vowed to leave his life of luxury in the palace, as well as his wife and child, to find a solution to all of the world's misery. He never awoke his wife or son to say goodbye; instead, he said his goodbyes under the cover of darkness before disappearing into the jungle. Siddhartha Gautama cut his long hair with his sword and changed into a plain robe — an ascetic's robe.

When Siddhartha Gautama chose to abandon his royal life in favor of an ascetic, he joined an entire community of men who had done the same. These guys, including Siddhartha Gautama, were looking for blissful liberation from individuality and life cycle — birth to death. His first teacher was Arada Kalama. Arada Kalama had over 30 disciples who were studying his philosophy. He instructed Siddhartha Gautama on training his mind to reach a state of emptiness or nothingness. It took a lot of patience to get to this point of mindful calm. However, Siddhartha Gautama recognized that this was not the salvation or deliverance he wanted, so he abandoned Arada Kalama's teachings and moved on to Udraka Ramaputra. Here, he was taught to concentrate on penetrating a world of his mind that was neither conscious nor unconscious. Once again, he was disappointed by what he discovered because he knew it was not true freedom.

Siddhartha Gautama studied and practiced different focus, philosophies and living a simple life devoid of personal comforts, wealth, and limited food. Over about 6 years, he followed these lessons and austerities with 5 companions. Since he took his activities seriously, Siddhartha Gautama seemed to be more dead than alive at times, a walking, breathing skeleton. During this time, he went to great lengths to deny himself daily necessities such as food, consuming only a single rice grain each day. He performed these penances because he wanted to elevate his mind to a higher level, one that was not reliant on his body, where his mind was free and freed from his body's needs — a level of utter focus and reality.

Siddhartha Gautama, still unable to find the bliss and salvation he wanted, abandoned his ascetic existence. When he abandoned asceticism, his five companions abandoned him, and Siddhartha left for a village searching for more substantive food. He met Sujata in the village, who gave him a jar of honey and some milk. Siddhartha drank the milk and ate the honey, feeling his strength and determination return. He bathed in the Nairanjana River before proceeding to the Bodhi tree, an ancient, holy fig tree with heart-shaped leaves. The Bodhi tree was later associated with Buddhism and was dubbed the "tree of enlightenment." Siddhartha Gautama spread out a mat under the Bodhi tree and sat cross-legged to reflect on what he had experienced.

Siddhartha Gautama had read so many holy books, listened to so many teachers, and taught so many different philosophies and strategies for attaining blissful liberation. So he sat under the Bodhi tree for six days, motionless and silent, thinking he had nowhere to turn to and no-one to depend on but himself. According to legend,

Siddhartha Gautama first saw the morning star on the sixth day. It was at this point that he attained nirvana or complete enlightenment. He knew without a doubt that everything he had been searching for had never really been lost. In reality, anyone could discover it. There was no need to struggle and live an exhausting life trying to find something that was never lost — the answers were all inside himself and each person. Siddhartha Gautama was 35 years old on this sixth day under the Bodhi tree. It was at this time that he became the Buddha — the Awakened One. The Buddha was also known as the Shakyamuni, the sage, intellectual scholar or philosopher, of the Shakyas. He is believed to have said upon awakening and reaching enlightenment:

"Wonder of wonders, this very enlightenment is the nature of all beings, and yet they are unhappy for lack of it."

The Buddha had reached a state of blissful liberation, deliverance from the reality around him, a realm of his mind that brought him the peace and happiness he sought with such determination. He relished his newfound freedom and tranquility for 7 weeks. He was not inclined to share his discovery with anyone else because he was uncertain about explaining it. But the story tells that Brahma, the chief of the 3,000 worlds, asked the Buddha to share his path to enlightenment with others, and the Buddha agreed. For approximately 45 years, the Buddha shared his knowledge with the world, creating a Sangha Buddhist community. He even visited his only son once more, who wound up joining the Sangha. The Buddha eventually passed away in Kushinagar.

Understanding the Concept of the Dalai Lama

What is the Role of a Dalai Lama?

The Dalai Lama is the head monk of Tibetan Buddhism and was historically in charge of ruling Tibet until the Chinese government took over 1959. Before 1959, his official residence was Potala Palace in Lhasa, Tibet's capital.

The Dalai Lama is a member of the Gelugpa Tibetan Buddhist tradition, the largest and most powerful Tibet.

The Dalai Lama's institution is a relatively new one. There have only been 14 Dalai Lamas in Buddhist history, with the first and second Dalai Lamas receiving the title posthumously.

According to Buddhist belief, the present Dalai Lama is a reincarnation of a previous Lama that chose to be resurrected to continue his valuable work rather than passing through the wheel of life. Tulku is an individual who chooses to be reborn indefinitely.

Buddhists assume that Gedun Drub, who lived from 1391 to 1474, was the first tulku in this reincarnation, and Gendun Gyatso was the second.

However, the title Dalai Lama, which means Ocean of Wisdom, was not bestowed upon him until his third reincarnation in the form of Sonam Gyatso in 1578.

Tenzin Gyatso is the new Dalai Lama.

How is a Dalai Lama Chosen?

Following the death of a Dalai Lama, it has historically been the Gelugpa Tradition's High Lamas and the Tibetan government's duty to find his reincarnation.

The High Lamas are looking for a boy born around the time of the Dalai Lama's death.

It can take two or three years to find the Dalai Lama, and it took four years to find the new 14th Dalai Lama.

The High Lamas will learn where the next reincarnation will be found in a variety of ways.

Dreaming

One of the High Lamas may dream about a mark or place to help the boy be identified.

Direction of Smoke

If the previous Dalai Lama was cremated, High Lamas would search in the direction of the smoke.

The Oracle Lake

High Lamas visit Lhamo Lhatso, a holy lake in central Tibet, and wait for a sign from the lake itself. This may be a vision or an indication of where to look for information. Tenzin Gyatso's home and village were found in a vision from this lake.

Once the High Lamas have found the home and the baby, they present the child with several artifacts that they had brought with them in preparation.

Among these artifacts are some objects belonging to the late Dalai Lama. Suppose the boy chooses objects belonging to the previous Dalai Lama. In that case, this is interpreted as proof, along with all of the other indicators, that the boy is a reincarnation.

This practice, however, is not set in stone, as Tenzin Gyatso has stated; if two-thirds of Tibetans wish to modify the method of determining the next reincarnation, this will be just as true.

The Dalai Lama's quest was traditionally restricted to Tibet, even though the third tulku was born in Mongolia. Tenzin Gyatso, however, has stated that if he is reborn, he will not be born in a country ruled by the People's Republic of China or any other country that is not secure.

Interestingly, Tenzin Gyatso has expressed doubts about whether he will be reborn at all, implying that the Dalai Lama's role might be over. However, once Tibet is reunited with its spiritual leader, it appears possible that the Dalai Lama will continue to exist.

The 14th Dalai Lama – Tenzin Gyatso

Tenzin Gyatso is Tibetan Buddhism's 14th Dalai Lama. He was born in 1935 and was recognized as Thubten Gyatso's reincarnation at a young age. Tenzin Gyatso was born Lhamo Dhondrub on July 6, 1935, to a peasant family in the Amdo province, in the village of Takster in northeastern Tibet.

The High Lamas of the Gelugpa tradition had been looking for the next Dalai Lama reincarnation for many years, but according to records, some incidents identified Lhamo as the correct boy.

The embalmed 13th Dalai Lama's face is said to have suddenly turned northeast. This, along with a High Lama vision while looking in the holy lake Lhamo Lhatso, suggested that Amdo was the village to seek. Also, the vision clearly showed a three-story monastery with a gold and turquoise roof, as well as another vision of a small house with unusual guttering.

A monastery at Kumbum in Amdo matched the High Lama description, and the house of Lhamo Dhondrub was found after a thorough search of the surrounding villages. At the time, Lhamo was about three years old. The search party went to his house and watched him without explaining why they were there. They returned a few days later with the formal purpose of carrying out the final exam.

They gave the child some objects, including a mala, rosary, and a bell from the late Dalai Lama. Lhamo immediately recognized the things, exclaiming, "It's mine, it's mine!"

He was enrolled in the local monastery and started his training when he was just over 5 years old. He was also educated by the highest monks in Lhasa, Tibet's capital city and his official residence. He was crowned at the age of 15 in 1950, just as tensions with China were escalating, but he continued to study until the age of 25, earning the highest honors available.

According to traditional maps, the young Lhamo Dhondrub, renamed Jamphel Ngawang Lobsang Yeshe Tenzin Gyatso, assumed leadership of a nation that was still a Chinese province.

China's political landscape was changing around 1950. There are plans in the works to formally annex Tibet to China. However, in March 1959, Tibetans took to the streets to demand the end of the Chinese rule. Thousands were killed as Chinese People's Republic troops suppressed the uprising.

Fearing that the Chinese government would assassinate him, the Dalai Lama fled from Tibet to India, where he was received by Indian Prime Minister Jawaharlal Nehru. Nehru authorized him to establish the Tibetan Government in Exile in Dharamsala, India. The Dalai Lama and the refugees who followed him established a community that promotes Tibetan language, culture, arts, and religion.

He is the first Dalai Lama to visit the West, and his charismatic demeanor has aided in gaining widespread support for Buddhism and the Tibetan resistance movement.

In 1989, he was awarded the Nobel Peace Prize for maintaining a non-violent approach with the Chinese government, despite knowing that many Tibetans would gladly engage in armed resistance to restore him to his status as their leader.

The Fragmentation of Buddhism and the Different Schools

The various Buddhist schools of thought that exist today arose after the Buddha's death (l. c. 563 - c. 483 BCE) in an attempt to perpetuate his teachings and respect his example. While Buddha has demanded that no leader be chosen to lead anything resembling a school after his death, this was ignored, and his disciples seem to have fairly quickly institutionalized Buddhist thought with laws, regulations, and a hierarchy.

There may have been a single vision of what Buddha taught at first, but differences about what constituted the "true teaching" resulted in division and the creation of three major schools:

- Theravada Buddhism (The School of the Elders)
- Mahayana Buddhism (The Great Vehicle)
- Vajrayana Buddhism (The Way of the Diamond)

Theravada Buddhism is the most ancient and claims to preserve Buddha's original vision and teachings. Mahayana Buddhism is said to have broken off from Theravada because it was too self-centered and had lost sight of the true vision; this school also claims to adhere to the Buddha's original teaching. The two schools may have originated simultaneously, but with different foci, from two earlier schools: the Sthaviravada (possible predecessor to Theravada) and the Mahasanghika (also given as Mahasamghika, considered by some the earlier Mahayana). However, the connection between these earlier and later schools has been questioned. Vajrayana Buddhism arose, primarily in Tibet, in reaction to what was seen as too many laws in Mahayana Buddhism and emphasized living the Buddhist walk naturally without regard to ideas about what one was "supposed" to do; it, too, claims to be the most authentic.

All three schools believe in the Buddha's Four Noble Truths and Eightfold Path, but they vary – often dramatically – how they want to follow that path. Objectively, none are considered more valid than the others, nor are the numerous minor schools that have formed, notwithstanding adherents' beliefs to the contrary. While non-adherents often view Buddhism as a uniform belief system, it is as diverse in practice as any other; however, theoretically, a modern-day secular Buddhist may engage in rituals with a religious Buddhist without consideration or dispute; both working toward the same basic goals.

Buddha preached his vision from the time of his awakening until his death at the age of 80, when he asked his followers not to choose a leader but to lead themselves. He also demanded that his ashes be interred in a stupa near a crossroads. Neither of these demands was met, as his disciples quickly formed a group with a leader and divided his remains among themselves, each deciding to position them in a stupa in a location of their choosing.

They held the First Council about 400 BCE, where they developed accepted Buddhist doctrine based on the Buddha's teachings, and the Second Council in 383 BCE, where the Sthaviravada school insisted on the observance of ten prescriptions in monastic discipline, which the majority rejected. At this stage, either the Sthaviravada school of thought left the group (known as the sangha), or the majority distanced themselves from the Sthaviravada and referred to themselves as Mahasanghika ("Great Congregation"). Both subsequent schools arose from this initial schism.

To compete with the more known belief systems of Hinduism and Jainism, these schools created an illustrious founding narrative for their founder and attributed several miracles to him. Nonetheless, Buddhism remained a minor sect in India until it was promoted by the Mauryan king Ashoka the Great (r. 268-232 BCE), who adopted the faith and began its spread. He sent missionaries to other countries, such as Sri Lanka, China, Korea, and Thailand, and Buddhism was embraced much more quickly in these places than in its home country.

Doctrinal variations, on the other hand, caused more schisms within the adherent group. These variations became more pronounced as the belief system became more institutionalized. Different canons of scripture emerged, some of which were accepted as valid while others were dismissed, and various practices arose in response to the scripture. The Pali canon, which originated from Sri Lanka, for example, maintained that Buddha was a human being who, despite being born with great spiritual strength, attained enlightenment by his own efforts and, when he died, he was set free from samsara and gained complete freedom from human affairs.

However, as Buddhism spread, the creator became revered as a transcendent being who had always existed and would always exist. Buddha's death was still regarded as his nirvana, a "blowing away" of all attachment and craving, but some disciples saw it as an elevation to an eternally abiding state, liberated from samsara, but still present in spirit. This belief and many others (such as the fact that the Buddha never existed physically, only as a kind of holy apparition) was held by the Mahasanghika school, which stood in stark contrast to Sthaviravada and, later, Theravada schools. While adherents preserved the Buddha's core vision, doctrinal differences such as this resulted in creating separate schools of Buddhist thought.

Although there were several schisms before establishing Theravada, Mahayana, and Vajrayana (the Mahasanghika school alone created three separate sects by c. 283 BCE), the Buddha is said to have predicted the separation of these schools from the original sangha in what is known as The Three Turnings. This idea is based on the Dharmachakra (a well-known Buddhist symbol of an eight-spoked wheel), representing the Eightfold Path, which is told by dharma, which is understood as "cosmic law" in Buddhism. The Dharmachakra has always been in motion and will continue to be so. Still, it was set in motion when Buddha gave his first sermon in terms of human acknowledgment. It would then make the first turn with Theravada Buddhism, a second with Mahayana, and a third with Vajrayana.

Theravada Buddhism (The School of the Elders)

This practice is part of the Eightfold Path and is influenced by the school's central figure, the sage Buddhaghosa (5th century CE), whose name means "Voice of the Buddha" because of his ability to understand and comment on Buddhist doctrine. They consider the Pali canon to be the most authentic, and they emphasize a monastic understanding of the Buddhist path in which the person seeks to become an arhat (saint), with no obligation to teach others the path to enlightenment. If one so desires, one can do so; however, unlike Mahayana Buddhism, the purpose is not to become a spiritual guide to others but to free oneself from samsara.

Theravada Buddhism is divided into a priesthood of monks and a community of lay people, with the monks considered more spiritually advanced than the common folk. Women are believed to be inferior to men and are not thought to achieve enlightenment until they are reincarnated as a man. Mahayana Buddhists may refer to the Theravada school as Hinayana ("little vehicle") but this is considered an insult by Theravada Buddhists because it implies that their school is not as important as Mahayana.

Mahayana Buddhism (The Great Vehicle)

Mahayana Buddhists called themselves the "Great Vehicle" either because they believed they had the true teachings and could bring the greatest number of people to enlightenment (as has been claimed) or because they emerged from the early "Great Congregation" Mahasanghika school and wished to distinguish themselves from it, albeit slightly. It was created 400 years after Buddha's death, most likely influenced by early Mahasanghika philosophy, and was streamlined and codified by the school's central figure, the sage Nagarjuna (c. 2nd century CE). It may have begun as a minor school before engaging with Mahasanghika, or it may have evolved independently without the influence of that school, but in any case, Mahayana is the most widespread and influential form of Buddhism in the world today, spreading from its initial acceptance in China, Korea, Mongolia, Japan, Sri Lanka, and Tibet to points all over the world.

According to the Mahayana school, all humans have a Buddha-nature and can achieve transcendent consciousness, becoming a Bodhisattva ("essence of enlightenment") who can lead others on the same path. Adherents strive for the state of sunyata, which is the awareness that all things lack inherent reality, nature, and enduring value - a mental clearing that allows one to understand the true nature of life. One becomes a Buddha after attaining this higher state, just as Buddha did. This transcendental condition is similar to how the Buddha regarded gods and spirits – as existing but incapable of providing any service to the person – but as a Bodhisattva, all women and men who have awakened can help others help themselves.

As with Theravada and all other Buddhism schools, the focus is on self-perfection and self-redemption – and no-one else can do the spiritual work required to liberate oneself from suffering. While Mahayana Buddhists regard Buddha as a deified being, the tenets do not allow anyone to seek assistance. According to Buddha's vision, belief in a creator god who listens to one's prayers is discouraged because it binds one to a power outside of oneself and sets one up for disappointment and anger when prayers go unanswered.

This is not to suggest that no Mahayana Buddhists pray directly to the Buddha; the practice of representing Buddha in statuary and sculpture, praying to these artifacts, and calling them holy - observed in Mahayana Buddhism - was introduced by the Mahasanghika school and is one of the many convincing reasons to believe the younger school evolved from, the older.

Vajrayana Buddhism (The Way of the Diamond)

Vajrayana Buddhism ("Diamond Vehicle") derives from the connection of enlightenment with unbreakable material. It is also known as the "Thunderbolt Vehicle," particularly in Tantric or Zen Buddhism, since enlightenment comes like a thunderbolt after putting in the necessary effort to perfect oneself. It is sometimes considered an offshoot of Mahayana Buddhism. It is even referred to as a sect of that school. Still, it actually borrows tenets from both Mahayana and Theravada Buddhism while incorporating its own innovation.

In both Theravada and Mahayana Buddhism, one chooses the path, recognizes the Four Noble Truths and the Eightfold Path as valid, and commits to a spiritual practice that will lead to enlightenment by renunciation unprofitable behaviors. In Vajrayana Buddhism, it is believed that one already has a Buddha-nature – everybody does, just as Mahayana believes – but that to completely awaken, one just needs to recognize this. To begin one's work on the road, an adherent does not need to give up bad habits like consuming alcohol or smoking right away; one just needs to commit to pursuing the path, and the temptation to indulge in unhealthy and destructive behaviors will gradually lose their allure. Rather than distance oneself from desire, one moves into and through it, shedding one's attachment as one progresses in the discipline.

The Vajrayana school of Buddhism, like Mahayana Buddhism, focuses on being a Bodhisattva who can then lead others. Since it was systematized in Tibet by the sage Atisha (l. 982-1054 CE), it is often referred to as Tibetan Buddhism. The Dalai Lama, who is sometimes referred to as the spiritual leader of all Buddhists, is officially just the spiritual head of the Vajrayana School of thought, and his beliefs are most closely aligned with this school of thought.

Chapter 2: A General Look at the Teachings of Buddha

The word Buddha means "The Awakened One," and it derives from the Sanskrit root budh, which means "to awaken." He is a man who has completely awakened as if from deep sleep to discover that his pain, like a dream, has come to an end. The historical Buddha, on the other hand, was a man like any other, but an extraordinary one; what he rediscovered was a way that everyone, if they are so inclined, can walk.

Gautama, the historical Buddha, was not the first Buddha. There had been those who had gone before him. He was not a deity, prophet, or another spiritual being. As we have seen, he was a human being who was conceived, lived, and died. An extraordinary human being who found a path to true wisdom, love, and liberation from pain. He rediscovered an ancient route to an ancient settlement, which had been hidden and forgotten. He could find the way out of poverty and into freedom through his own efforts, and those who have followed him have kept the path open.

The Buddha did not teach that the Universe was formed by a god. He pointed to a great law or Dharma that runs through all. True wisdom and compassion, and thus liberation from misery, can be attained by living by this law. Suffering, on the other hand, can only be resolved by confronting and living through it. In the words of the Buddha, 'I teach suffering and the way out of suffering.' The following are fundamental Buddhist doctrines:

The Chain of Causation

This vital doctrine teaches the interconnectedness of all things, specifically the law of Karma and the process by which we construct a world of misery for ourselves and others and the opposite; the way to live that eliminates suffering for all and leads to liberation.

- Change
- Suffering
- No "I"

The first, Change, emphasizes that nothing in the universe is constant or permanent. We are not the same people we were ten years - or even ten minutes - ago, in terms of physical, emotional, or mental health. As for changing beings on shifting sands, living as we do makes it impossible for us to find long-term stability.

Concerning the second sign, we have already seen how Suffering's experience inspired the Buddha to embark on his great spiritual journey, even though suffering is a poor translation of the original term, dukkha. Dukkha denotes the unsatisfactory and incomplete existence of life in general. However, this does not imply that Buddhists believe life is all about misery. Buddhists believe that happiness exists in life, but that it is fleeting and that even in the most fortunate of lives, there is pain. Happiness, like anything else, is subject to the law of transition and impermanence.

The third Sign, No I, is a little trickier.

Buddhists claim that there is nothing eternal or unchangeable in humans, no spirit or self in which a safe sense of 'I' can anchor itself. The definition of 'I' is fundamentally false, attempting to create itself in an inconsistent and ephemeral series of elements. Consider the classic analogy of a cart. A cart can be disassembled into its basic parts, including the axle, wheels, shafts, sides, and so on. The cart is no longer there; all that remains is a jumble of parts. Similarly, 'I' is composed of various elements or aggregates (khandhas): shape (rupa-khandha), feeling-sensation (pleasant, negative, neutral), awareness (sanna-khandha), volitional mental activities (sankhara-khandha), and sense consciousness (vinnana-khandha).

The Noble Four Truths

- The Noble Truth of Suffering
- The Noble Truth of Origin of Suffering
- The Noble Truth of Suffering
- The Noble Truth of the Way Leading to Suffering's Cessation: The Noble Eightfold Path

Buddhism starts with the reality of pain. However, before we can do anything about it, we must first understand what is causing it, which is the profoundly ingrained sense of 'I' that we all have. As a result, we constantly strive to obtain pleasurable experiences while avoiding uncomfortable ones to find ease and comfort, and generally to exploit people and circumstances to be the way 'I' want them to be. And because the rest of the world does not always agree with what I want, we frequently find ourselves going against the grain and being hurt and frustrated as a result. Therefore, suffering can be alleviated by transcending this powerful sense of 'I,' bringing us into greater harmony with things in general. The Noble Eightfold Path is how this is accomplished.

The Noble Eightfold Path

- Right Understanding
- Right Thought
- Right Speech
- Right Action
- Right Livelihood
- Right Effort
- Right Mindfulness
- Right Concentration

The Wheel is Dharma's sign, with eight spokes representing the Noble Eightfold Path.

Right Understanding is relevant at the start because we can't make any kind of beginning if we can't see the Four Noble Truths' reality.

Right Thought inevitably stems from this. 'Right' in this context means by the facts: with the way things are, which might vary from how I would like them to be.

Right Thought, Right Speech, Right Action, and Right Livelihood entail moral restraint in the form of not lying, cheating, committing violent actions, or making one's living in a way that is detrimental to others.

Moral restriction not only promotes general social cohesion, but it also helps us regulate and reduce our sense of 'I.' The more we allow 'I,' like a selfish boy, to have its own way, the bigger and more unruly it becomes.

Next, Right Effort is necessary because 'I' thrives on idleness and wrong effort; some of the most violent offenders are the most energetic people, so effort must be sufficient to the diminution of I, and in any case, if we are not willing to exert ourselves, we cannot expect to accomplish anything at all in either the spiritual or the physical sense.

The first stage toward liberation from suffering is represented by the Path's final two stages, Right Mindfulness or consciousness, and Right Concentration or absorption. Being conscious and at one with what we are doing is central to proper living; this practice can take many forms, but the formal practice is known as meditation in the West. An individual sits cross-legged on a cushion on the floor or upright in a chair in the most basic Buddhist meditation type.

He or she observes the rise and fall of the breath silently. If ideas, desires, or urges emerge, he or she simply experiences them as clouds in the sky, coming and going without dismissing them on the one side or being swept away into daydreaming or restlessness on the other. It should be learned under the supervision of an instructor, just as the Buddha did.

The Three Fires of Buddhism

- Desire
- Anger
- Delusion

'Your house is on fire, burning with the Three Fires; there is no dwelling in it,' said the Buddha in his famous Fire Sermon. The house he is referring to here is the human body, and the three fires that are burning in it are (1) Desire/Thirst, (2) Rage, and (3) Delusion. They are various forms of energy that are referred to as "fires" because, if left unchecked, they can rage through us and harm us as well as others! However, when properly calmed by spiritual training, they can be turned into genuine humanity's genuine warmth.

'Not to do any evil; to cultivate good; to purify one's heart - this is the teaching of all the Buddhas,' in general.

While Buddhists value virtues such as loving-kindness, humanity, patience, and giving, it is possible that they value wisdom and compassion the most. The concept of ahimsa, or harmlessness, is inextricably linked with compassion – the compassionate desire to do no harm to all people, including animals, plants, and the environment as a whole. Buddhism emphasizes self-sufficiency in all aspects, and the Buddha himself advised his followers not to believe without asking but to try it for themselves. Buddhism is also a very rational faith that seeks to help people live peacefully.

Buddhists also strive to consciously uphold Buddhist values in their daily lives. The ultimate aim of all Buddhist practice is to achieve the same awakening that the Buddha attained by the active transformation of the heart and passions and letting go of I.

Chapter 3: The Foundation of Buddhism - The Four Noble Truths

Buddhism's main aim is to bring an end to suffering and rebirth. 'Both in the past and now, I set out just this: suffering and the cessation of suffering,' said the Buddha. Although this formulation is pessimistic, the purpose has a positive aspect since the way to end misery is to satisfy the human capacity for goodness and happiness. Nirvana is said to be achieved by someone who completes this full state of self-realization. Nirvana is Buddhism's summum bonum—the ultimate and highest good. It is a philosophy, as well as an experience. It provides a specific view of human fulfillment and contours and shapes the ideal life as a philosophy. It becomes incarnate in the individual who seeks it over time as an experience.

It should be obvious that nirvana is wanted, but how can it be obtained? Part of the response is suggested by the discussion in the preceding chapters. We know that Buddhism emphasizes living a virtuous life; thus, living morally appears to be a requirement. Some academics, however, disagree. They contend that gaining merit by good deeds ultimately hinders the attainment of nirvana. They argue that good deeds generate karma and that karma ties one to the cycle of rebirth. Since this is the case, the reason, karma - along with all other ethical considerations - must be overcome before nirvana can be attained. This point of view has two flaws. The first is to clarify why, if moral behavior is a hindrance to nirvana, the texts constantly encourages the performance of good deeds. The second challenge is understanding why those who achieve enlightenment, such as the Buddha, continue to live morally exemplary lives.

A solution to these issues may be to argue that living a moral life is just one aspect of the ideal of human perfection that nirvana represents. As a result, while virtue (silo, Sanskrit gita) is an important component of this ideal, it is insufficient on its own and must be balanced by something else. Wisdom is another necessary aspect (patina, Sanskrit: prajna). In Buddhism, 'wisdom' refers to a profound metaphysical interpretation of the human condition. It necessitates insight into the essence of truth, which can only be obtained through long contemplation and deep thought. It is a form of gnosis, or direct apprehension of reality, that deepens over time and eventually reaches full maturity in the Buddha's complete awakening.

Nirvana is thus a synthesis of virtue and wisdom. In metaphysical terms, the relationship between them can be articulated as follows: virtue and wisdom are both 'essential' conditions for nirvana, but neither is sufficient: only when the two are present together are the necessary and sufficient conditions for nirvana found. An early text compares them to two hands washing and purifying each other and makes it abundantly clear that an individual who lacks one or the other is incomplete and unfulfilled.

A later chapter delves further into the philosophy of nirvana.

Given that knowledge is the necessary counterpart of virtue, what does one need to know to become enlightened? The reality must be learned, which the Buddha perceived on the night of his enlightenment and later detailed in his first sermon delivered in a deer park near Benares. This sermon refers to the Four Noble Truths, which are four interconnected propositions. A medical metaphor is often used to describe their relationship, and the Buddha is compared to a physician who has discovered a cure for life's ills. First, he diagnoses the illness, then discusses its cause, then decides whether or not a cure exists, and finally, he describes the treatment.

According to The Truth of Pain, suffering (dukkha, Sanskrit: dukkha) is an inherent part of life, and the human condition is essentially one of 'dis-ease.' It refers to various types of suffering, starting with physical or biological experiences, such as birth, illness, old age, and death. While these often include physical discomfort, the deeper issue is the inevitability of repeated birth, illness, aging, and death for oneself and loved ones, lifetime after lifetime. Individuals have no control over these realities. Despite developments in medical science, their physical natures make them vulnerable to illness and accident; in addition to physical pain, the Truth of Suffering refers to emotional and psychological forms of distress, such as "grief, sorrow, lamentation, and despair." This can also be more difficult to overcome than physical suffering: few lives are free of sadness and sorrow, and there are many crippling psychological disorders, such as persistent depression, from which full recovery can never be achieved.

The Truth of Suffering *(Dukkha)*

The Truth of Suffering refers to a more subtle form of suffering that could be defined as 'existential.' This is exemplified by the phrase, 'Not getting what one wants is pain.' The type of misery envisioned here is the anger, dissatisfaction, and disillusionment felt when life does not live up to our standards, and things do not go as planned. The Buddha was not a grim pessimist, and he learned from his own experience as a young prince that life can be enjoyable. The problem is that the good times do not last; they fade away sooner or later, or one becomes bored with what once seemed novel and full of hope. In this context, dukkha has a more abstract and prevalent meaning: it implies that even though life is not difficult, it can be unsatisfying and unfulfilling. 'Unsatisfactoriness' expresses the essence of dukkha better than suffering in this and many other ways.

The Truth of Suffering, near the end of the formulation, implies a more profound explanation of why human existence can never be ultimately satisfying. The phrase "the five elements of individuality are suffering" refers to teaching articulated by the Buddha in his second sermon (Vin.i.13), which divides human existence into five components: the physical body (nripa), sensations, and emotions (vedana), cognitions (saiiiia), character characteristics and dispositions (sarikhara), and consciousness or sentiency (viiblana). There is no need to go into depth about each of the five variables because the key point here is not what the list contains or does not contain. The doctrine, in particular, makes no mention of a soul or self, identified as an eternal and permanent spiritual essence. By taking this stance, the Buddha distinguished himself from the orthodox Indian religious tradition known as Brahmanism, which held that each person possesses an eternal soul (Annan) that is either part of, or identical with, a metaphysical absolute known as brahman (a sort of impersonal godhead).

According to the Buddha, there is no evidence for the presence of either the personal soul (atman) or its celestial equivalent (brahman). Instead, he took a more realistic and scientific approach, more akin to psychology than theology. He defined human existence as composed of five elements, similar to how an automobile is composed of its wheels, transmission, engine, steering, and chassis. Unlike science, he believed that a person's moral identity - what we could term the individual's "spiritual DNA" - survives death and rebirth. However, in claiming that the five factors of individuality are misery, the Buddha also said that human nature cannot provide permanent happiness because the five factors doctrine demonstrates that the person has no real heart. Since humans are made up of these five continually changing elements, suffering will inevitably occur sooner or later, just like an automobile will eventually wear out and break down. Suffering is therefore woven into the fabric of our being.

The Buddha's vision of the first three of the four signs - the old man, the ill man, and the corpse - supplies the pan for The Truth of Suffering's content, as does his understanding that life is rife with suffering and unhappiness of various kinds. Many people who come into contact with

Buddhism find this evaluation of the human condition to be negative. Buddhists typically respond that their faith is neither negative nor positive but rather rational and that the Truth of Suffering simply presents life's facts objectively. If the presentation seems gloomy, this is due to the human inclination to avoid painful realities and 'look on the bright side.' Without a doubt, this is why the Buddha observed that the Truth of Suffering was exceedingly difficult to comprehend. It is analogous to accepting that one has a serious illness, which no-one wants to accept, but once the disorder is understood, there is no hope of a cure.

Given that life is misery, how does this suffering come about? The Truth of Arising (samudaya), the Second Noble Truth, states that suffering emerges from craving or 'lust' (talha, Sanskrit tma). Craving fuels misery in the same way that wood fuels a fire: in the Fire Sermon (S.iv.19), the Buddha described all human experience as being "ablaze" with desire. Since it eats what it feeds on without being satisfied, fire is an apt metaphor for desire. It spreads quickly, attaches to new things, and burns with the agony of unsatisfied longing.

It is a desire that induces rebirth in a powerful addiction to life and fun experiences. If the five aspects of individuality are compared to a vehicle, desire is the fuel that propels it forward.

While rebirth is typically thought to occur from life to life, it often occurs from second to second as the five factors of individuality shift and interact; motivated by the desire for pleasurable experiences. Person continuity from one life to the next is simply the product of the cumulative momentum of desire.

The Truth of Arising *(Samudaya)*

According to the Truth of Arising, craving or thirst expresses itself in three ways: thirst for sensual gratification, thirst for knowledge, and thirst for power. This manifests as a desire for pleasure through the senses, such as the desire to encounter good tastes, feelings, odors, sights, and sounds. The second is a desire to live. This relates to our deep instinctual desire to move forward through new lives and experiences. The third way craving expresses itself is as an urge to kill rather than possess. This is the dark side of desire, embodied as the desire to negate, dismiss, and reject what is undesirable or unwanted. The drive to kill can also lead to self-deprecation and self-negation. When directed at oneself, low self-esteem and thoughts such as 'I'm no good' or 'I'm a failure' manifest this attitude. It can lead to physically self-destructive actions, such as suicide, in extreme cases. Physical austerities, which the Buddha ultimately opposed, can also be seen as an example of this urge to self-negation.

Is this to say that all desire is bad? We must proceed with caution before reaching this conclusion. Although the English word 'desire' is sometimes used as a translation for raffia, it has a much broader semantic range. It has a more limited definition and denotes desire that has been perverted in some way, typically by being excessive or incorrectly guided. Its primary goals are normally sensorimotor stimulation and enjoyment. However, not all desires are of this kind, and Buddhist sources also use the word chanda to describe desire in a more optimistic light. Possessing positive dreams for oneself and others (such as achieving nirvana), hoping for others' happiness, and wishing to leave the world a better place than one finds it is all examples of positive and wholesome wishes that do not count as tapha.

Right desires strengthen and liberate, while wrong desires restrain and bind. To demonstrate the distinction, we might use smoking as an example. A chain smoker's urge for another cigarette is raffia because its aim is just short-term gratification. A desire like this is compulsive, limiting, and cyclical: it leads nowhere but to the next cigarette (and, as a side effect, to ill health). A chain smoker's urge to quit smoking, on the other hand, would be a noble desire because it would break the cyclical cycle of a compulsive negative habit and improve health and well-being.

Talha represents the 'three roots of evil' listed above in the Truth of Arising: greed, hate, and illusion. Since craving only leads to more craving, the cycle of rebirth continues indefinitely, and individuals are born again and again. This is discussed in depth in the teaching known as 'origin-in-dependence' (paticca-samuppida, Sanskrit: pratitya-samutpada). This doctrine describes how craving and denial contribute to regeneration in a twelve-stage progression. Rather than delving into the twelve steps, it is more important to understand the basic concept, which relates not only to human psychology, but also to reality in general.

At its most simple level, the doctrine can be summarized as the argument that any effect has a cause: in other words, all that exists is dependent on something else (or on several other things). According to this viewpoint, all events emerge as part of a causal chain, and nothing occurs separately in and of itself. As a result, the universe is seen as a complex network of interconnected causes and effects rather than a series of more or less static objects. Furthermore, just like the human being can be reduced to its constituent parts with nothing left over, all phenomena can be reduced to their constituent parts with nothing 'important' in them.

The Buddhist universe is defined primarily by cyclic change: at the psychological level, in the never-ending phase of desire and gratification; at the personal level, in the sequence of death and rebirth; and at the celestial level, in the creation and destruction of universes. Underlying all of this is the cause-and-effect concept outlined in the doctrine of origination-independence, the ramifications of which were formulated deeply in later Buddhism.

The Truth of Cessation is the Third Noble Truth (nirodha). This Truth declares that when the craving is eliminated, suffering ends, and nirvana is achieved. As the story of the Buddha's life will remember, nirvana takes two forms: the first happens during life, and the second occurs after death. At the age of 35, the Buddha achieved 'nirvana-in-this-life' while sitting under a tree. He died at the age of 80, entering 'final nirvana,' from which he would not be resurrected.

'Nirvana' simply means 'quenching' or 'blowing out' in the same way as a candle's flame is blown out. But what exactly is 'blown out?' Is it a person's spirit, ego, or identity? It cannot be the soul that is blown out because Buddhism rejects the existence of such a matter. The self or one's sense of identity does not vanish, although nirvana does entail a fundamentally transformed state of consciousness free of the obsession with me and mine. The triple fire of greed, hate, and illusion that leads to rebirth is, in effect, extinguished. Indeed, the most basic nirvana-in-this-life concept is "the cessation of greed, hate, and illusion" (S.38.1). Nirvana-in-this-life is a psychological and ethical truth, a transformed state of mind marked by calm, deep spiritual joy, compassion, and refined and subtle consciousness. The enlightened mind is free of negative mental states and emotions, such as doubt, concern, anxiety, and fear. Saints in many religious traditions display some or all of these virtues, and ordinary people, to varying degrees, possess them as well, although imperfectly formed. An enlightened individual, such as a Buddha or an Arahant, is thought to fully possess them.

The Truth of Cessation *(Nirodha)*

What happens to such an individual after death? Problems of comprehension emerge in conjunction with final nirvana. Rebirth ends when the flame of craving is extinguished, and an enlightened person is not reborn. So, what really happened to him? In the early sources, there is no definite answer to this issue. The Buddha once said that wondering where an enlightened one goes after death is akin to wondering where a flame goes when it is extinguished. Of course, the flame hasn't 'gone' anywhere; it's just that the process of combustion has come to an end. Removing craving and ignorance is analogous to removing the oxygen and fuel that a flame needs to burn. However, the picture of the flame blowing out should not be interpreted as implying that the final nirvana is annihilation: the sources make it very clear that this would be incorrect, as would the inference that nirvana is the everlasting life of a personal soul.

The Buddha discouraged speculation about the existence of nirvana and instead stressed the importance of striving for it.

Those who posed speculative questions about nirvana were likened to a man wounded by a poisoned arrow which, instead of taking the arrow out, insists on learning trivial details about the man who shot it, such as his name and clan, how far away he was standing, and so on (M.i.426). In keeping with the Buddha's unwillingness to elaborate on the topic, early sources characterize nirvana in primarily negative terms, such as "the absence of desire," "the extinction of hunger," "blowing out," and "cessation." There are a few optimistic epithets, such as 'the auspicious,' 'the decent,' 'purity,' 'peace,' 'reality,' and 'the further shore.' Certain passages imply that nirvana is a transcendent truth that is 'unborn, unoriginated, uncreated, and unformed' (liana 80), but such formulations are difficult to understand. In the end, the essence of final nirvana remains a mystery to those who have not seen it. What we can be certain of is that it signifies the end of pain and rebirth.

The Fourth Noble Truth of the Path or Way (maggot, Sanskrit: marga) describes how one progresses from sarrmaro to nirvana. Few people pause to consider the most satisfying way to live amid the hustle and bustle of daily life. Questions of this kind preoccupied contemporary Greek and Indian thinkers, and the Buddha had something to say about it. He believed that the highest level of life resulted in the creation of virtue and wisdom, and the Eightfold Path lays out a way of life to bring these to fruition.

The Truth of the Path *(Magga)*

The Eightfold Path is known as the "middle way" because it guides people between a life of indulgence and life of harsh austerity. It is made up of eight elements divided into three categories: Morality, Meditation, and Wisdom. These describe the criteria of human well-being and show that there is space for human flourishing. The moral virtues are perfected in the division known as Morality (silo), and the intellectual virtues are established in the division known as Wisdom (paha). How about meditating?

While the Path consists of eight factors, they should not be viewed as stages to be passed through on the way to nirvana and then abandoned. Instead, the eight elements demonstrate how Morality, Meditation, and Wisdom can be practiced regularly. Right View entails first accepting Buddhist teachings and then experiencing their experiential validation. Making the Right Decision entails making a significant commitment to cultivating the Right Attitudes. Telling the facts when thinking thoughtfully and sensitively is what Right Speech entails. Right Action entails refraining from wrongful bodily acts, such as murder, theft, or wrongdoing about sensual pleasures. Right Livelihood entails not working in a job that causes damage to others. Right Effort entails taking care of one's emotions and maintaining optimistic mental states. Mindfulness in its purest form entails maintaining continuous consciousness. Right Meditation entails cultivating deep mental relaxation levels through various strategies that focus the mind and incorporate the personality.

In this sense, the Eightfold Path practice is a modeling process: the eight factors show how a Buddha will live, and living like a Buddha gradually transforms one into one. Thus, the Eightfold Path is a path of self-transformation: an intellectual, emotional, and moral restructuring in which an individual is reoriented from selfish, narrow goals to a horizon of possibilities and opportunities for fulfillment. Ignorance and selfish desire are resolved by the pursuit of wisdom (paha) and spiritual virtue (silo), the cause of the arising of misery is eliminated, and nirvana is attained.

Chapter 4: Walking the Noble Eightfold Path

The Noble Eightfold Path is one of the primary teachings of the Buddha. The Noble Eightfold Path is visually represented by the Buddhist symbol of the dharma wheel. The dharma wheel is one of the oldest Buddhist symbols. It is believed that the Buddha set the wheel into motion upon the delivery of his first sermon teaching about Buddhism. The wheel symbolizes the cosmic order of things, which we know is part of the dharma - a cosmic law and order. A wheel is always in motion, always moving; hence, it symbolizes the constant movement of the cosmic order of life.

You will remember that Buddhism is the philosophy of seeking liberation from the suffering of life. The Noble Eightfold Path is a guide to show you how to end the suffering of every life. Almost the entire philosophy of Buddhism draws from this path. Its very essence is found within so many of the Buddha's teachings, so many of his beliefs spread to his disciples, and then they spread throughout the world. The 8 practices of the Noble Eightfold Path are as follows:

Right Understanding

Understanding the way things really are, understanding the truth of things, knowing that every action has a consequence. This practice teaches you how to truly understand the world around you, a deep understanding that only comes with a pure and developed mind.

Right Thought

Knowingly giving up your material home and taking on the life of simplicity, modesty, love, and kindness, extending your thoughts of love and kindness to every living creature. This practice teaches you about releasing the bad while retaining the good. It teaches you to spread goodness to everyone you come across in life.

Right Speech

Never lie, never gossip or slander another in a way that brings hatred and disharmony, never speak ill, rudely, maliciously, or abusively of another person. This practice teaches you to use kind, gentle, friendly, and useful words, words that have meaning, words that have the truth. If you cannot say something useful, keep a "noble silence."

Right Action

Never kill or injure another, never steal, give up material things, give up illegitimate sexual acts. This practice teaches you to conduct yourself in a moral, peaceful manner, with honor. It also teaches you to lead by example, to show others how to conduct themselves in the same honorable manner.

Right Livelihood

Only have just enough to live, to sustain a living, never work in a trade that harm's another living creature. This practice teaches you how to live with just enough so that you made abandon greed and envy. It also reinforces war and other professions that bring with them evil and harm to others.

Right Effort

Letting go of the negative, embracing the positive, ridding yourself and others of evil, creating positive, good, and wholesome states of the mind. This practice teaches you to, essentially, let go of the bad while holding on to the good. It also encourages you to show others how to eliminate evil from their lives.

Right Mindfulness

Be mindful of the Buddhist teachings, always conscious of your actions, always aware of your feelings, thoughts, and ideas. This practice teaches you to always know what is going on within yourself and give careful thought to your actions. This goes hand-in-hand with letting go of the negativity and embracing the good in life. It teaches you to be always conscious and aware at every moment so that you will always put forth kindness, love, and happiness.

Right Concentration

Practice meditation, develop your mindfulness, train and discipline your mind. This practice teaches you the stages of meditation. This first stage is when you discard all unwholesome thoughts from your mind, feeling only joy. The second stage is when you, essentially, clear your mind of any mental activities, teaching it to become still and tranquil while you still feel the happiness and joy. The third stage teaches you to let go of the joy while still remaining happy. The fourth stage of meditation is when you release even the feelings of happiness, when your mind is a pure place, feeling and thinking nothing, only being aware.

There is no right or wrong numerical order to follow the practices of the Noble Eightfold Path. The list is just that — a list of the practices. The primary goal of a burgeoning Buddhist is to develop each practice at the same time. Each practice builds upon other practices. As a Buddhist, you must work to develop the practices within yourself as far as you are capable of doing. Each practice is going to take time to nurture and develop. Do not expect immediate results — Buddhism's path is a long one, one that is full of many, many steps.

The Eightfold Path is a path that is followed, practiced, and developed within yourself. Your path is not going to be the same as your fellow Buddhist's path. Each path is individual, each practice developed at your own pace, within your own skills. The Eightfold Path teaches you self-discipline, self-development, and self-purification. It is not a religious path upon which you will participate in a ceremony or a form of prayer or worship. This is the Buddha's path, the very one that he followed, to reach freedom, peace, and perfect happiness — to reach nirvana.

…

Chapter 5: Suffering, Karma, Nirvana and Reincarnation According to Buddhism

The law of karma is a central tenet of the Buddhist worldview. In a nutshell, karma believes that deliberate deeds have consequences for the agent, both in this life and in future lives; in reality, karma causes rebirth.

Buddhists regard the law of karma as a manifestation of dependent arising (paicca-samuppda), the law of cause and effect, according to which all that happens occurs as a result of particular circumstances.

"Not in the sky, nor amid the sea,
Nor by hiding in a mountain cave,
No place on earth is to be found,
Where one might escape one's wicked deeds."

What is Suffering in Buddhism

To live is to suffer because neither human nature nor the world we live in is perfect. Throughout our lives, we must experience physical suffering, such as pain, illness, injury, tiredness, old age, and, finally, death and psychological suffering, such as grief, anxiety, anger, disappointment, and depression. While there are various degrees of misery and pleasant experiences in life that we view as the opposite of suffering, such as ease, comfort, and happiness, life in its entirety is imperfect and incomplete because our world is impermanent. This means that we will never be able to keep what we aspire for forever, and just as happy times pass, so will we and our loved ones.

Attachment to transient objects, as well as ignorance of them, is the source of misery. Transient things include the actual objects around us and concepts and, in a broader context, all objects of our experience. Ignorance is described as a lack of understanding of how our minds become attached to impermanent objects. Suffering is caused by greed, ambition, ardor, the pursuit of riches and glory, the desire for fame and recognition, or, in a nutshell, longing and clinging. Since our attachment artifacts are transient, their loss is unavoidable, and so suffering is unavoidable. Attachment objects also include the concept of a "self," which is a delusion because there is no enduring self. We call "self" merely an imagined entity, and we are merely a part of the universe's never-ending becoming.

Via nirodha, one may achieve the cessation of pain. Nirodha refers to the dissolution of sensual craving and mental connection. The third noble reality reflects the notion that misery can be alleviated by achieving dispassion. Nirodha extinguishes all ways of attachment and clinging. This means that suffering can be alleviated by human intervention by eliminating the source of the suffering. Attaining and perfecting dispassion is a multi-level mechanism that culminates in the state of nirvana. Nirvana is the state of being cured of all fears, troubles, complexes, fabrications, and thoughts. For those who have not achieved nirvana, it is incomprehensible.

There is a way out of misery — a gradual self-improvement course outlined in greater detail in the Eightfold Path. It is the path that connects the two extremes of excessive self-indulgence (hedonism) and excessive self-mortification (asceticism), and it leads to the end of the rebirth period. The latter distinguishes it from other routes that are merely "wandering on the wheel of being" because they lack a final object. The path to liberation from suffering may take several lifetimes, during which each human rebirth is subject to karmic conditioning. Craving, ignorance, delusions, and their consequences will fade gradually as you move along the road.

The Three Categories of Dukkha

Buddhist teachings reveal the three types of Dukkha:

- The first is the *Dukkah-dukka,* or the dukkha of painful experiences. This category comprises both the mental and physical sufferings associated with birth, aging, illness, and death. It refers to the pain experienced from what does not give pleasure.
- The second is the *Viparinama-dukka* or the dukkha of the transforming nature of all beings. The experience of feeling frustrated because you are not getting what you expected or desire best describes this category.
- The third is the *Sankhara-dukkha,* or the dukkha of conditioned experience. This is characterized by one's "basic insatiability" prevalent in all forms of life and all of existence because all forms of life are ever-changing, never permanent, and without an inner substance or core. In other words, it refers to constant desire in a way that one's satisfaction and expectations can never really be met.

Multiple Buddhist teachings emphasize that life in the mundane world is dukkha. It does not just include birth, aging, illness, and death, but also feelings of grief, pain, worry, and despair. Being separated from one's beloved is dukkha just as much as being associated with one's enemy is. Whenever one does not acquire what one wants, it is dukkha.

The Five Clinging-Aggregates is an important Buddha concept about dukkha as well. These are:

Form or Matter (Rupa)

Any sentient being or object comprises four elements: earth, water, fire, and wind.

Sensation or Feeling (Vedana)

This refers to the experience of a being's senses, which can be enjoyable, unenjoyable, or neutral.

Perception (Samnjna)

It is the mental and sensory process that notices, acknowledges, and labels. One uses perception to notice the feeling of happiness and anger, the size and color of plants and animals, and so on.

Mental Formations (SamskaTa)

These are every single kind of mental imprints and conditioning caused by any object. They also encompass any process that causes one to act on something.

Consciousness (Vijnana)

This refers to one's awareness of any object and the ability to distinguish its parts and features. Different Buddhist teachings explain Consciousness as:

Having a knowledge of something or discernment (according to Nikayas/Agamas).

A set of interconnected discrete acts of discernment that changes quickly (according to the Abhidhamma).

The foundation of all experience (according to some Mahayana texts).

In a nutshell, one can safely say that suffering can be found anywhere and everywhere. You experience it whenever you feel attached to anything, be it your thoughts, words, actions, body, mind, loved ones, surroundings, and so on. The only way to be free from it is to follow the Buddha's advice, and it is to practice the Noble Eightfold Path.

Now that you have gained further insight into Suffering's Buddhist concept, you might be interested in learning more about Karma.

What Does Nirvana Stand For in Buddhism?

The Pali word Nibbana (nirvana in Sanskrit) was coined by the Buddha to describe the highest state of profound well-being that a human being can achieve. The mind awakens from insanity, freed from slavery, cleansed all its defilements, is fully at peace, suffers no more, and is no longer reborn.

According to Gautama Buddha, nirvana is a state of transcendental happiness that can be achieved during or at the end of life. Nirvana roughly translates as "to snuff out," as in "to extinguish a fire." This has no negative connotation in Buddhism; rather, it refers to transitioning to another plane of life by extinguishing the flames of desire, illusion, rage, and hate. Nirvana is known as Nibbana in Pali.

Attaining nirvana is inextricably related to the philosophy of karma, in which the soul's accumulated deeds and attachments become the explanation for the soul being stuck in an endless cycle of reincarnation. Following the Buddha's teachings (the Noble Eightfold Path) leads to liberation from rebirth and nirvana attainment. This experience is aptly defined by His Holiness the Dalai Lama as a "state beyond sorrows."

The other characteristic of nirvana is Bodhi, or enlightenment, which is a full realization of the true nature of truth. A Buddha is anyone who has attained or resides in Bodhi.

Nirvana Day is observed by some Buddhists to mark the Buddha's achievement of nirvana. On February 18th, Parinirvana Day is traditionally observed. On this day, Buddhists visit monasteries or temples. It is a day to ponder one's life and how to move toward achieving nirvana. Buddhists often remember the recent deaths of family members and close friends as a way to accept the inevitability of death. More precisely, in a person who achieves nirvana, the flames of greed, hate, and delusion - toxic unconscious mental and emotional dispositions that cause people to harm themselves and one another and cause suffering - have been extinguished (nibbuta). The common interpretation is that nirvana means "blowing out" the flames, but it is more likely that the word refers to extracting fuel from a fire so that it goes out, or freeing the fire from its sticking to its fuel. In the early tradition, there are two meanings of the word: nirvana as the radical psychological transformation undergone by Siddhartha Gautama under the Bodhi tree at the age of 36, and parinirvana ("complete" nirvana) as the more mysterious transformation experienced when the Buddha died between two sal trees at the age of 80. When the toxic flames were extinguished, he reached nirvana, lived for 45 years teaching others how to do the same, and then entered parinirvana with the final passing away of his body and mental aggregates (feeling, perception, dispositions, and consciousness).

One of the most difficult aspects of the word nirvana is that it can be used negatively and positively. Too much focus on the negative meaning (such as the absence of delusion) risks misconstruing it as nothingness, while too much emphasis on the positive definition (such as the highest happiness) will contribute to the desire to think of it as an eternal truth. Both were discouraged by the Buddha, who said that there are no adequate philosophical means of communicating nirvana.

Each of the two major Mahayana schools approached the subject differently. The Madhyamaka emphasized the negative mode, emphasizing the term's ineffability and dismantling the notion of the sharp contrast between nirvana as an exalted state and samsara as a fallen universe. The philosopher Nagarjuna contended that nirvana and samsara (literally, the "flowing forward" from one life to the next) are indistinguishable - it is only one's mistaken point of view that distinguishes them.

Yogacara thinkers like Vasubandhu preferred to emphasize the optimistic aspects of nirvana. Building on the concept of a transpersonal "storehouse consciousness," they coined concepts like bodhicitta, dharma-kaya, buddha-nature, and suchness. Tibetan forms of Buddhism appeared to follow suit, speaking of the "great bliss" of nirvana being available through tantric practice.

As Buddhist teachings spread across East Asia, both outward and inward orientations evolved. The Tiantai and Hwayan schools created grand integrated cosmological structures centered on nirvana as the central concept of the cosmos, while Chan and Zen practice emphasized seeing one's true inner self. A legacy of masters embodied nirvana's experience, transmitting their inexpressible realization through imaginative and spontaneous responses to ordinary circumstances.

Understanding Karma

The inevitability of karmic effects has played a significant role in how conventional Buddhism has portrayed its ethical teachings. Killing, stealing, lying, and other evil deeds are
bad karmas that will result in rebirth in an unfortunate human condition or in hell. Good deeds, on the other hand, such as generosity (particularly giving to Buddhist monks), generate merit and lead to rebirth in a nice human condition or in Heaven. Although Western Buddhists are aware of the conventional teachings on karma, they are more likely to

interpret the rule of karma in a psychological sense, as a reminder that good actions will result in nice experiences in this life, and bad actions will result in unhappiness.

When western Buddhists discuss the rule of karma, they often have only one meaning in mind: the psychological meaning of karma. In Buddhism, the rule of karma amounts to this: deliberate acts of body, voice, and mind have psychological effects for the agent, so that good actions bring positive experiences in their wake, while bad actions bring negative experiences. For example, if I make a habit of going to the monastery and giving food and money to the monks and nuns, my generosity would have the following consequences: I feel happier because my attention has been guided beyond myself; I feel motivated because by giving to the monks has brought me into contact with Dharma practitioners,
and I feel my life is more meaningful because my kindness has brought me into general communication with the sangha.

If, on the other hand, I make a habit of falsifying my tax returns and stealing packets of coffee from work, the following consequences will occur: I will feel unhappier because of the edge of anxiety that HMRC will catch up with me, or the kitchen manager at work will
notice my theft; I will feel more anxious because I need to be careful who I am honest with, partic

ularly at work; and I will feel my life is a struggle because I will falsify my tax returns.

The psychological interpretation of the karma rule is critical for understanding how ethical behavior has positive implications and leads to a happier, more integrated sense of self. This is the strongest foundation for further advancement on the Buddhist path.

Buddhist ethics is founded on the axiom that "actions have consequences," but a good action has good consequences for all, not only for oneself. The law of karma is derived from the ethical axiom, but the psychological implications for oneself should not be the only consideration for one's behavior.

However, for many of us, the prospect of greater happiness can serve as a reminder to be healthy.

However, when conventional Buddhists discuss karma law, they typically have something other than the psychological sense of karma in mind, which I will refer to as the universal meaning of karma.

In its more traditional sense, the law of karma is a philosophy of universal moral justice: intentional acts of the body, voice, and mind would have felt consequences in this life or, more possibly, in future lives.

According to the universal law of karma, if I make a habit of going to the monastery and giving food and money to the monks and nuns, such generous acts create merit, which is similar to a positive balance on a cosmic balance-sheet, and which, after I die, will result in my having a pleasant rebirth, perhaps in a wealthy family.

If, on the other hand, I cheat on my taxes and steal the coffee, I will accrue demerit, which is a negative weight on the celestial balance-sheet that, after I die, will result in a less fun rebirth, maybe in a family of thieves, or among tax-collectors or coffee-growers, or perhaps in a hell-realm.

The universal law of karma is a part of Buddhist cosmology; as a result of their karma, beings pass between the different realms of life – human, spiritual, hellish, and animal.

Because of universal impermanence, all beings continually emerge and pass away, and the consequences of both good and bad behavior only last for a limited time until they are depleted.

As a result of the rule of karma, the gods will fall, and the inhabitants of hell may find their way back into the world.

This universal karma is a divine justice mechanism in which moral deeds do not disappear into obscurity, but rather embody themselves in the fabr ic of life, their moral merit preserved until the very world rewards and punishes good - and evil - doers.

Karma as a Process

According to the Buddha, karma is not an all-around determinant, but rather a part of the factors that affect the future, with other factors being circumstantial and about the nature of the being. It moves in a fluid and dynamic way rather than in a mechanical, linear manner. In fact, not all factors in the present can be attributed to karma.

Be careful not to define karma as "fate" or "foreordination." Karma is not some form of godly judgment imposed on beings that did good or bad things. Rather, it is the natural result of the process.

In other words, doing a good deed would not automatically entitle you to a future of happiness, and vice versa. After all, while certain experiences in your life are due to your past actions, how you respond to them is not yet determined. Of course, such responses to circumstances would then lead to their own consequences in the future.

Karma as Energy

All beings constantly change due to karma. For every thought, action, and word being produced, a kind of energy is released in different directions into the universe. These energies can influence and change all other beings, including the being that sends the energy.

The main reason why Buddhists emphasize the value of understanding karma is the fact that your knowledge of it will help you free yourself from samsara. Once you have recognized that every single intention and action you do may affect your future, you become more mindful of your thoughts, words, and deeds. Ultimately, we are the ones in control of our future, but if we continue to be ignorant of our choices, then it would naturally lead to more suffering.

It's a good idea to try to think of all of our actions having karmic value because if you switch over to that philosophy, you start to head in a more positive direction. Your suffering, and whether you continue in the endless circle, really depend upon what you learn in this life.

Another valuable exercise is to try and work on the positivity of your energy. This can be worked on in all kinds of environments. When you encounter a situation that tempts you to use negative energy, try to look at it from another stance and think of how you can use positive energy instead. The karma that lies in our actions often comes from the actions taken and the negative energy shared. Thus, it will always work in your favor, be honest in your dealings with others, and raise your energy level above any negative experiences you may encounter.

As you learn to discipline the mind, you also learn to control the karma that happens in your day-to-day life, and that's huge. That means that you limit your suffering and can live with that high energy positively that influences those around you to stay positive regardless of what difficulties they are faced with. The inner voice of calm that can be the voice of criticism and anger helps you to become a better person. That is important, but you need to ensure that your solutions are not so closed-minded that they impinge upon others' thoughts and energies.

A Piece on Reincarnation

When you think of the word reincarnation, what comes to mind?

Most people would think of it as the idea of dying and then resuming life once more on earth, but this time in a different form. For instance, if you were human in this lifetime, then depending on how good or bad you were, you could be reincarnated into a life of a king or a cockroach.

Unfortunately, such a misunderstanding of reincarnation has caused most people to shun all the Buddha's other pertinent teachings. This problem may be because many have been misinterpreting many of Buddha's eighty-four thousand parables.

It should be noted that Buddha adopts a teaching style that is appropriate to the abilities of the learner, and during times when the people were accustomed to the simple way of life, he resorted to explaining his teachings in the form of stories. The Buddha had used the concept of being reincarnated into an animal to explain how one's ignorance ensnares one in the cycle of life and death. However, some who did not understand such a metaphor took the meaning literally.

It is important to remember that reincarnation — rebirth — does not literally equate to physical birth. Experiencing rebirth does not mean that your consciousness is transferred to the fetus of a dog after death.

The True Meaning of Reincarnation

The term "reincarnation" (sometimes called "rebirth" in English books about Buddhism) does not have a direct translation in the languages of Sanskrit and Pali. Instead, traditional Buddhist teachings describe the concept using various terms, but all represent the crucial step in the never-ending cycle of samsara. The terms Pali and Sanskrit are also termed *samsara which* means "wandering about," and it refers to the universal process of being reborn repeatedly.

One such Buddhist term is *pubarbhava,* which literally translates to "becoming again." Another is *punarjanman,* which means "reborn." Yet another one is *punarmrityu,* which translates to "re-death." Sometimes the simple word *bhava* - becoming — is used. However, the Pali and Sanskrit word for being born into the world in any way is *jati,* which literally means "birth."

One interesting paradox is in many people who do not fully understand the Buddhist concept of reincarnation. It is that one's soul transfers from one's dying body into a new one. However, the truth is that Buddhists do not actually believe that there is such a thing as a permanent "soul" within living beings.

According to Buddhism, a being — especially a human — is a combination of its thoughts, emotions, and perceptions that it uses as forms of energy to interact with the universe. In return, the universe sends back a reaction to these energies – *karmaphala* - that would cause a change in the person. Many Buddhists believe that such a transformation signifies that the person has become "born again" in the world of *samsara,* and the cycle continues.

The Ten Realms of Being

Concerning reincarnation in traditional Buddhism, there exist the Ten Realms of Being. The Ten Spiritual Realms represent the ten conditions of life that living beings experience each moment of their lives.

The Ten Realms of Being comprises Six Lower Realms of Desire, namely Hell, Hunger, Brutality, Arrogance, Passionate Idealism, and Rapture. The remaining are the Four Higher Realms of Nobility, namely Learning, Absorption, Bodhisattvahood, and Buddhahood. Buddhist modernists usually interpret these ten realms as states of mind instead of viewed in the literal sense.

Now, let us take a closer look at each of the ten realms. Perhaps you could even discover which one you are in right now.

The Six Lower Realms of Desire

Most sentient beings are trapped within these six lower realms. However, they do not move from one realm to another in a linear fashion, but more dynamically depending on their karma and other factors.

Here are the six lower realms of desire: 1. Hell

In traditional Buddhism, this realm is called the *Naraka*. In it, you experience a complete state of blind hostility. You feel as if you do not have the free will to choose how to act, in the sense that you seem ensnared in the circumstances beyond your control.

Those trapped in this realm are the ones who find it difficult to hold back their frustrations, anger, and hatred. They have the constant urge to destroy themselves and other beings around them. They see everything as threatening and hostile, so they feel claustrophobic toward their surroundings. Be warned, for it is difficult to escape from this realm.

Hunger

Traditional Buddhists call this realm the *Pretas* or the world of the Hungry Ghosts. Those who are in this realm are the beings that have never-ending appetites coupled with extreme possessiveness. Such negative qualities affect their thoughts and actions toward the source of their desire, be it power, fame, wealth, pleasures of the flesh, and so on. This "addiction" is never satiated; what is more, the level of desire heightens as soon as the being satisfies it.

Beings who are in this realm find it almost impossible to instill self-discipline. Their pursuit of pleasure affects them to the point where they no longer care for other beings' welfare. This is a state that people can easily understand today and is something that individuals can work on to correct the sense of need. Many learn from their own experience that the core of their need is a manifestation of lack within their lives and does not add to the character. However, the lesson is a hard one to learn.

Brutality

This particular realm falls under the Buddhist World of the Animals. It is where the trapped being's thoughts and actions run on pure instinct, with no sense of morality. This means the being does not have sound reasoning and judgment.

Beings in the Brutality realm only live for the present moment, but not how the Buddha teaches mindfulness. Rather, they take advantage of others for selfish reasons, not unlike how predators stalk and kill their prey in the wilderness. They also manipulate others to gain their favor and use them for personal gain. Again, one can work their way out of this state by understanding their own weaknesses and by learning to overcome them. Changes in someone's life may signal a change of direction, which is needed to rise from this state, where the lack of morality is at the base of the problem.

Arrogance

In traditional Buddhism, this realm is described as the World of the Demigods or the Asuras. Beings trapped here are too engrossed in paranoid jealousy, the obsession with winning, and paralyzing selfishness. Another distinctive quality of such beings is their constant desire to be on top in life aspects they consider important.

Although having such traits in the modern world may be considered beneficial, in the long-term, it destroys the being. This is because they value their own beliefs and ego more than the welfare of others. Being too competitive also holds the being back from being compassionate toward others because they are considered contenders. It is good if you have things that you excel at, but you need to know the difference between being gifted and using the gift for the betterment of mankind and keeping the glory for yourself, seeing yourself as being the focal point. When you are gifted and accept that the gift you have can help others, you overcome the ego's part in the equation.

Passionate Idealism

In traditional Buddhist teaching, this realm falls into the world of Humans. It is one where the beings have developed advanced thinking skills and discriminating awareness. The common trait in this realm is in being too ambitious with one's ideals.

While this presents some benefits, especially as it can help motivate one to attain Enlightenment, it also leads to suffering due to attaining perfection. Similarly, we criticize people who try to be perfectionists because their self-criticism holds them back from achieving enlightenment. This sense of everything having to be perfect can stunt spiritual growth, which is not measurable and hard for perfectionists to understand. For example, when learning meditation, the perfectionist may try too hard and yet achieve very little. They need to let go of the need to be perfect in an ever-changing world, accept the changes that happen, and become flexible toward them.

Rapture

Traditional Buddhists associate this realm with the Buddhist world of the gods or the Devas. In this realm, which is sometimes referred to as the Heaven Realm, the beings experience short-lived but strong feelings of pure pleasure.

It cannot be avoided that beings only stay in this realm for a short time because the rapture feeling is momentary. Eventually, the being would then go back to a lower realm.

The Four Higher Realms of Nobility

The Four Higher Realms represent the traditional Buddhist tenet that sentient beings must exert all willpower and motivation to let go of their desires in the mundane world to understand nature's realities and become their true selves.

The seventh and eighth realms — Learning and Absorption — are referred to as the "Two Vehicles" in Mahayanist Buddhism. This means that when a being finds himself in these realms, he is on the way to reaching the noblest realms.

However, because of the presence of desire and the focus on the self, specifically to increase one's wisdom and gain insight, then the being is still within the samsara.

Learning

In traditional Buddhism, this realm is represented by the Sravakabuddha World or the realm of the Enlightened Disciples of a Buddha.

In this realm, beings are in a state where they seek knowledge of the Truths and self-improvement by becoming learners. Specifically, they seek the guidance of a mentor or *guru*. Such guidance can be obtained from texts and other pre-recorded information if not coming from the guru himself.

To come out of the lower realms and into this one, the aspirant should instigate the motivation to learn and have an open mind toward the world's true nature. This is a positive state because you are receptive to the lessons you are being taught. You are also questioning and will find that gurus will give you examples to aid your understanding of life. This is a time when you may be reading a lot or going to classes to widen your knowledge and understanding of Buddhism.

Absorption

This particular realm in traditional Buddhism is the World of the Pretvekabuddha, or "a Buddha on their own."

Beings who have reached this realm seek the truth based on their own observations and concentration. Typically, those in this realm have discovered that while external sources are indeed useful (as in the Learning Realm), one's own learning experiences are truly superior. Therefore, beings that are in this realm have chosen to seek wisdom and truth through internal discernment.

This will apply to those who have learned to meditate and have the self-discipline to take that learning a step further. Once you do begin to learn and understand, this stage is one where you may improve your meditation to such an extent that you gain great understanding from it. You will be able to concentrate sufficiently to gain much from all that you are taught.

Bodhisattvahood

When the being has reached this realm, traditional Buddhists would state that he is in the World of the Bodhisattva.

As mentioned in the previous sections, the Bodhisattva wish to become Buddhas to help other sentient beings find Enlightenment. Beings who have the compassion to commit themselves to help other beings reach this realm. They experience pure bliss from having reached Enlightenment and going on with their life guiding learners who are on their way. Being almost a teaching stage, this higher state would apply to people willing to help others understand Buddhism's teachings. This may apply to teachers within a Buddhist community who have proven awareness and help others gain that same sense of awareness. There is no ego here. There is simply the need to pass on the learning to others to experience the most from Buddhism studies.

Buddhahood

The Enlightened One, The Buddhas, reside in this realm. Reaching this realm means experiencing the pure, everlasting joy that cannot be influenced by any circumstances.

The Buddhas are free from all desire and suffering. Their wisdom, compassion, and loving-kindness know no bounds. Because sentient beings who have reached this realm are so rare, it is not easy to describe. Generally speaking, it is no longer possible for those who have reached Buddhahood to descend to any of the lower realms because their happiness is no longer attached to external sources.

However, the Buddha explained that all living beings are capable of reaching this realm. This realm does not depend upon anything other than reaching nirvana or total understanding and enlightenment, and that's what people seek when they meditate, just as the original Buddha did. This is what people aim for through meditation and is the purpose of the journey into Buddhism.

I hope that this chapter has shed light on the Buddhist concept of reincarnation for you. At this point, you can reflect on certain aspects of your life, such as the realm in which you think you find yourself now. This helps you to aim higher — not for ambition's sake, but to improve who you are and to help others on their road too.

By understanding reincarnation, you can also be more mindful of your intentions, thoughts, and actions. Keep in mind that you then transport yourself to a different realm for each choice you make in this life. To attain the higher levels, you may choose to seek constant inspiration from the Buddha's teachings and practice self-discipline and mindfulness. This means teaching yourself to meditate and be mindful that the world around you is forever changing. You should recognize the changes in yourself and improve upon your weaknesses as a student of Buddhism. There are always people who are willing to assist you in your journey, but you need to have confidence in the people you choose to help you on this journey.

Chapter 6: The Current State of Buddhism

The Age of Information - our time - is when the world and its people are interconnected. More discoveries in science and technology seek to answer life's questions and solve many problems every day. People use the internet to access a limitless amount of data on practically any topic their minds could think of. It has also enabled one to create communities despite staying in one spot and to converse with anyone from any part of the world.

Yet, as the people in our time continue to surge through increasingly complex discoveries and innovations, one question remains the same: how much do we really know about ourselves? Are we slaves to desires and self-centeredness? On the other hand, are we still capable of upholding such timeless virtues as generosity and kindness?

Such reflections have led many toward the path that the first Buddha took over two thousand years ago. However, Buddhism in our time, including its principles, culture, and rituals, is not only tolerant, but actually adjusts to the needs of those who seek it. This is what makes it so relevant and pragmatic in modern society.

Using Buddhism as a Moral Compass

The concept of *karma* details how your choices regarding thoughts, words, and actions influence you and everything around you. However, Buddha's teachings do not just stop there. Rather, they show you how you can become more mindful of this responsibility so that you can lead a purposeful and truly happy life.

The best part is the Buddha's teachings do not just let you figure things out for yourself. Instead, it provides you with the Four Noble Truths to help you reflect deeply on what causes your suffering, and with the Noble Eightfold Path to enable you to solve such a problem. When you have that compass to follow, you have a huge amount of information to help you find your direction in life. The Noble Eightfold Path is simple for people to understand as the basis for living their lives. Although much has changed since the original Buddha's time, taking note of the Noble Eightfold Path and studying how it relates to your life helps you become more in tune with yourself. Your meditation practice helps you understand your own reactions to life and helps you understand the self-discipline used in Buddhism to stay within the path given by the original Buddha.

Embracing Buddhism as a Lifestyle

Another reason modern man has openly accepted the Buddha's teachings and practices are how it positively influences one's way of life. Buddhist concepts, such as the Five Precepts, Meditation, and Mindfulness make so much sense to the modern mind, even if one does not acknowledge spirituality.

The ability to exercise free will when heeding the Buddha's advice adds to this ancient discipline's appeal in the modern world. Unlike much of the world's dogmas, Buddhism emphasizes one's volition and encourages one to put experience before accepting Dharma.

There are plenty of other ways to view the role of Buddhism in our time. Through learning and experiencing it, you too can construct your own perspective of it. Now, you might want to ask yourself, "Why am I drawn to Buddhism? Which part of its practices and teachings are relevant to my life in modern society?" You might be surprised by what you can reflect on by giving yourself some time to answer these questions.

When you learn how to meditate, you also learn how to be in the breath. This means learning deeper breathing techniques that help you to remain focused in the now. Mindfulness uses all of the senses to be in the moment, rather than avoiding it by letting the mind drift to the past or future and thus lose the opportunity to enjoy the now. The breathing techniques also have value from a health perspective since most human beings use very little lung capacity when they breathe. When you learn to breathe in the way used during meditation, you enable your bodily functions to work better because the sympathetic nervous system responsible for many functions in your body can distribute the oxygen around your body.

You are also taught the importance of posture, and that's where yoga comes in very useful, as this is one of the first lessons learned. The body's posture helps in meditation because you are taught by gurus or teachers to position yourself so that the body's energy centers can receive the freedom needed to feel all of the joy that Buddhism can impart. Blocked energy paths, otherwise known as Chakras, need to enable energy to pass through them, and these are located along the length of the spine, this meaning that posture is vital to the flow of energy. If you have never thought of this, it may be worthwhile looking at a chart of the Chakras to understand their significance, and yoga teachers will make you conversant with these chakras and their uses when you go through a yoga class.

They help your energy to flow correctly, but they have other functions as well. For example, when you meditate, the idea is to open the third eye or see things you would not normally see. This includes the use of intuition and intuitive thought. Other chakras are located along the spine in the neck, heart, navel, and base of the spine, and the crown chakra, located at the top of the head. The movements and the breathing exercises you are introduced to during yoga exercises help keep these channels open. They have great significance to your levels of concentration and your ability to meditate.

Buddhists today learn all about the significance of the process of meditation and the discipline entailed. In a material world, it's very hard for people to go through the process of learning, although those who do come to a better understanding of life through their studies. Learning from gurus or yoga teachers, Buddhists go through the different breathing and meditation processes to reach that higher state with the Nobel Eightfold Path practice.

In our time, people have developed the habit of worrying and being anxious. The figures produced by health authorities show that medical experts are looking for alternatives to traditional medicines to help with what is a seeming epidemic. Many hospitals and medical facilities in Europe are now introducing patients to mindfulness classes to help stem the suffering without long-term medication. In fact, there are books written by the Dalai Lama, in conjunction with medical experts, who compare the values of the Buddhist to those of people who do not practice Buddhism and are interested in the way that the philosophy can be used to help alleviate the suffering of people in today's world. So far, the results have been astounding, and more and more people are turning toward the Buddhist philosophy, even without initially understanding what that meant to their everyday lives. By taking up meditation and yoga classes, they have values instilled that lead them to further explore the Buddhist way of life.

Buddhist centers across Europe and the United States are making inroads introducing students to the Nobel Eightfold Path in conjunction with mindfulness and meditation classes. Having attended centers in Europe, Buddhism's approach is open to all, and Buddhists are very welcoming to those seeking answers to their questions. The training done within Buddhist centers in France and in the United Kingdom encourages the study of philosophy hand-in-hand with teaching students the benefits of each of the paths taken when choosing to use philosophy as a way of life.

BUDDHISM BEGINNERS GUIDE: BUDDHA'S TEACHING FROM THE DALAI LAMA

Chapter 7: The Core Practices of Buddhism

Throughout the centuries, Buddhism practices have been transforming based on the people who continue to uphold them. In fact, how the practices are adopted is based on the culture of different societies.

Yet, one thing remains the same, and it is that the core values of Buddhism are preserved. Such virtues are being strong-willed, generous, kind, and selfless are universally accepted and timeless. Help you to become stress and anxiety-free at the least, and how they can help you stay motivated as you follow the Noble Eightfold Path.

Mindfulness Meditation

When you talk about Buddhism, you cannot avoid mentioning the concept of meditation. It is the core of the practice. Additionally, scientific studies can attest to its mental and physical benefits. Meditation is a generally accepted and widely recommended way to reduce stress in everyday life, improve cognitive and emotional intelligence, and increase positive thinking.

Much can be said about the different types of Mindfulness Meditation; you can conduct further research on your own on the following practices:

Theravada Buddhism Meditation

- Anapanasati
- Satipatthana
- Metta
- Kammatthana
- Samatha
- Vipassana
- Maha Sati
- Dhammakaya

Vajrayana and Tibetan Buddhism Meditation

- Ngondro
- Tonglen
- Phowa
- Chod
- Mahamudra
- Dzogchen
- The Four Immeasurables
- Tantra

Zen Buddhism Meditation

- Shikantaza (sitting meditation)
- Zazen
- Koan
- Suizen

Chanting and Mantras

Another common practice in Buddhism is chanting. Buddhist monks in different parts of East and Southeast Asia practice chanting regularly to improve their concentration and reflect deeply on Buddhist concepts.

Buddhists modernists use phrases in their spoken language to create mantras that help *them sink deeper into their meditative state as well.*

You may be familiar with the "Om," a sacred mantra that Buddhists chant at the start of all mantras. According to ancient Hindu texts, Om is the eternal sound in the past, present, and future. It embodies birth, life, and death, and it is used and heard every day. Interestingly, it is said that by chanting "Om," the vibrations it causes helps relax the body and mind.

There are also centers whose gurus give individual chants to students based upon the year, time, and place of birth, and these are personal to the student.

Chanting is found useful in many ways because it allows the student to concentrate on a given thing rather than allowing the mind to wander. Although this was not the specific purpose of mantras, it helps to cut out unnecessary thought processes that help the student meditate more successfully. It also helps the student with breathing since some mantras are used in rhythm with the breathing and help the student to deep breathe and to chant the mantra on the outward breath.

Vegetarian or Vegan Lifestyle

While it must be noted that the first Buddha himself never mentioned anything against the consumption of meat, many Buddhists choose to live the vegetarian or vegan lifestyle.

One of the main reasons for this is the cardinal principle of harmlessness, or *ahimsa,* which states that all living beings have divine spiritual energy; therefore, by harming another being, one is harming the self as well.

Some Buddhists who choose to eat meat do so only out of necessity. For instance, those living in cold climates can only survive on a diet rich in fat and protein. In such cases, the Buddhists would then choose only the meat of ethically-raised animals. In other words, the animals lived a full and relatively happy and free life and were slaughtered most humanely and painlessly for their meat.

Ultimately, the decision to choose your diet rests in your hands, as the Buddha himself explained. Of course, no-one is exempted from eating meat's karmic results, especially if the living being was slaughtered specifically for you. This is worthy of note since Buddhist monks are often given food, and there is a story about a Buddhist monk who was extremely hungry. He was given a chicken plate and looked forward to eating it until he was told that the chicken had been slaughtered specifically. In this case, he was not permitted to eat it since this goes against Buddhist belief, and he was considered the cause of the killing.

As you can see, many, if not all, of Buddhism practices can easily be incorporated into the modern lifestyle. It is up to you how you perceive and practice these rituals each day. After all, it is only through experience that you can truly witness the benefits of these practices.

Apart from that, you may also incorporate yoga into your daily life, which I have explained in detail in a later chapter.

Chapter 8: Learning to Practice the Five Precepts of Buddhism

"The perfection of upasaka Precept is to abstain from killing, stealing, sexual assault, lying, and taking intoxicants," says Chapter 33 of the Samyuktagama Sutra. The Five Precepts are essential for upasakas and upasikas. While there are different precepts for monastics and laypeople, it is important to remember that all precepts are based on the Five Precepts. As a result, the Five Precepts are also known as the "Foundation Precepts."

Why is it Important to Follow Precepts?

Taking refuge in the Triple Gem is the first step in studying Buddhism, while following the precepts is the process of putting what you've learned into practice. After taking shelter in the Triple Gem, all Buddhists should follow the precepts because they form the basis of all virtuous acts and the universal norm for the human race. Embracing precepts is equivalent to students adhering to school rules or citizens adhering to common law in society. The only distinction is that school rules and the law are external constraints, whereas Buddhist precepts are a form of self-discipline and internal regulations. Accidents can occur if a driver on a smooth expressway fails to obey traffic laws.

Similarly, suppose an individual does not follow the precepts. In that case, he runs the risk of violating the rules and attracting problems in his life. As a result, adhering to the precepts is necessary for a Buddhist.

The Five Precepts Broken Down

"Never Involve Yourself in Killing"

Not killing entails not causing damage or ending the lives of others. This involves not killing any humans, cockroaches, mice, or insects, among other things. Since Buddhism is an anthropocentric religion, this precept is primarily aimed at not killing another human being because it is an unforgivable and significant infringement (Prajika), and repentance will not lessen the seriousness of the consequences of this violation. Although killing insects is still a crime (Duskrta), it is less serious than killing a human.

Since Buddhism teaches that life is an accumulation of time, wasting time or destroying some kind of resource is considered a killing. Since the formation of materials or substances necessitates time and effort, wasting time wastes shared resources and is considered a form of killing.

The primary aim of no killing is to increase our compassion. "Eating meat kills the seed of love, and a meat eater's every move will terrify all beings due to their bodily smell of meat," according to the Nirvana Sutra. As a result, the primary reason Buddhists practice vegetarianism is to cultivate compassion and loving-kindness. Plants may appear to have life, but they only have biological reactions, while animals are conscious, so consuming plants is not considered killing.

"Do Not Cheat or Steal"

No cheating entails not infringing on the property and possessions of others. To put it plainly, stealing is taking something that does not belong to oneself (whether privately or publicly owned) without permission, and robbery in broad daylight is also a form of theft. Stealing is a breach of a fundamental and essential principle. Taking public utensils and stationery for personal use or borrowing without returning is not a breach of the precept, but it is considered an impure act in Buddhism, and the effects of cause and effect must be faced. Of all the precepts, not cheating is one of the most difficult to follow.

"Refrain From Sexual Acts of Misdeed"

No sexual assault entails never engaging in sexual acts outside of a husband-wife relationship. Rape, prostitution, bigamy, seducing someone other than your marriage partner, trading human beings, interfering with the happiness of other people's families, and all other unethical sexual relations are all breaches of this precept. An individual who secretly loves someone but never acts on it might not have violated this precept; however, if the mind is thinking impure thoughts, s/he will not be living a free life, since the object of taking precepts is to purify one's body and mind.

Sexual violence is the spark that ignites an unsettled culture. Suppose a married couple does not engage in sexual exploitation. In that case, their relationship will be content and harmonious, and society's moral standard will be upheld.

"Refrain From Being Dishonest"

No lying entails refraining from using frivolous terms, such as lying, slandering, blunt language, and words that cause conflict. Exaggeration is also a breach of this Buddhist precept. In general, lying is classified as Major Lies, Minor Lies, and Convenience Lies.

Major Lies - People who claim to have attained enlightenment or spiritual powers but do not have them have violated this precept seriously. Another significant violation of this precept is criticizing the four Buddhist disciples, particularly the bhiksus and bhiksunis.

Minor Lies - bearing false testimony, misrepresenting, concealing the facts, or fabricating are all examples of minor lying.

Convenience Lies - This is known as good-intentioned misrepresentation. For example, a doctor can withhold information from a terminally ill patient to preserve the patient's emotional well-being.

"Stay Away From Intoxicants"

No intoxicants entail abstaining from alcohol and abstaining from any stimulus or substance that causes one to lose conscience or engage in unethical behavior. Marijuana, cocaine, amphetamine, sniffing glue, morphine, and other drugs, for example, must not be used.

The first four of the Five Precepts are laws against bad acts since they constrain behaviors that can lead to sins or transgressions. Not consuming alcohol is one of the Buddhist's Five Precepts since, although it is not a sin in and of itself, it is a major cause of lack of self-discipline and the commission of a crime, so this final precept is a law against actions that which impede the well-being of others.

According to the Mahavibhasa Sutra, a layman in India stole a chicken from his neighbor after consuming alcohol (a breach of the no-stealing precept) and then killed it for food to go with the alcohol (a violation of the no killing precept). When his neighbor began looking for her chicken, the man lied to her, claiming that he had not seen it (a breach of the no lying precept). At the same time, he noticed how attractive this neighbor was, so he sexually assaulted her (a violation of the no sexual misconduct precept). Drinking dulls one's sense of guilt and conscience, and drinking violates the precepts of murdering, stealing, sexual assault, and lying. As a result, it is important to refrain from alcohol.

Buddhism is a faith that emphasizes wisdom, and abstaining from alcohol allows one to stay sober, clear-headed, and wise.

The Overall Meaning of the Five Precepts

Even though there are five distinct precepts, their overarching concept is not to offend anyone. S/he will be free if he or she does not offend anyone but instead respects them. For example, no killing means not endangering other people's lives; no cheating means not invading other people's property; no sexual assault means not infringing other people's honor and integrity; no lying means not endangering other people's good name; and no drinking or using intoxicants means not endangering one's own intelligence and therefore not endangering others.

It is a common misconception that following precepts entails binding oneself down, so some would say: "Why should we follow precepts? It's just a burden!" The truth is that if we look at the individuals who are incarcerated, we will see that they have all broken one or more of the Five Precepts. Murder, sexual assault, and disfigurement, for example, are all violations of the "No Killing" precept.

The "No Cheating" precept is violated by corruption, embezzlement, stealing, burglary, robberies, kidnapping, and abduction. The "No Sexual Misconduct" precept is violated by rape, prostitution, seduction, and bigamy. The "No Lying" precept is violated by libel, slander, breaching a vow, falsifying facts, and intimidation. The "No Intoxicants" precept is violated by drug selling, drug use, drug trafficking, smoking, and consuming alcohol. A person's right has been taken away because of a violation of these precepts; thus, upholding these precepts is often a way of abiding by the common law.

Those who follow the Five Precepts and have a good understanding of these precepts will experience true freedom. As a result, the true sense of precepts is freedom rather than a burden.

It is widely held that if the precepts are violated, they become unavoidable; thus, there would be no violations if no precepts are observed. Even if a person violates a precept after taking it, they may feel ashamed and repent. As a result, the sin will be less serious, and there will always be a chance to achieve enlightenment. People who are unwilling to follow the precepts, on the other hand, may not repent if they violate the precepts and will live in the Three Evil Realms (hell, hungry spirits, and animals) and will never become a Buddha. Furthermore, not following the precepts does not mean that the precepts are not broken when something bad is done, since one is always guilty of the crime and must bear the effects of cause and effect.

Furthermore, if we do not kill but protect lives, we will have health and longevity; if we do not steal but give generously to the poor and needy, we will have wealth and be honored; if we do not commit sexual misconduct but respect other people's honor and integrity, we will have a fortunate and harmonious family; and if we do not lie but praise others, we will have a good reputation.

Chapter 9: Understand the Soul of Light and Enlightenment

When a human being has satisfied his basic needs — food, water, shelter, security, and so on — he begins to wonder about the purpose of existence or the essence of life. The Buddha himself had reflected on this, especially as he may have been a noble whose basic needs were fully satisfied.

After attaining enlightenment, the Buddha then began sharing his reflections with others. His teachings were then compiled into what is now the Dharma, and its purpose is to help those who are searching for the essence of their own lives and ultimately attain Enlightenment.

Of course, this does not mean everyone should live life in the exact same way. Rather, it means reaching your own unique highest potential in the same way the Buddha did when he attained Enlightenment.

So, how do you begin your path towards self-actualization? According to Buddhist teachings, you can find it by helping others, by cultivating the Four Divine Abodes, and by applying the Six Perfections in your life.

Aid Others

Compassion is the humane quality of recognizing other living beings' suffering and the desire to assist them in overcoming it. Buddhism teaches compassion, and it teaches people to appreciate life in general. Out of love, the Buddha wanted to assist others in their journey to enlightenment.

To find the essence in life in this aspect, you may begin to feel responsible for other beings, especially those in a more difficult situation than you are. Perhaps you can help others by volunteering with a local charitable group or using your talents.

Practicing the Divine Abodes

Meditation is the recommended way to cultivate the Four Divine Abodes, namely:
- Loving-kindness,
- Compassion,
- Sympathetic bliss, and
- Equanimity.

To do that, here are the steps that you can take. Keep in mind that you can always adjust this method to suit your preferences based on your experience of it:

Spend some time in a quiet and happy position focusing on one of the Four Divine Abodes.

For example, if you are going to mcditate on loving-kindness, consider how to explain this sensation. Try to accept this as part of who you are, and by meditating on them, you can discover that your meditation has real meaning and that you are getting closer to knowing what enlightenment is.

Consider a person in your life who can easily make you feel this quality.

If you are meditating on loving-kindness, you might be thinking about a loved one for whom you have a deep affection. These are frequently the people who bring out the best of us. You can see what it's like to bring these values into your life through their behaviors and their trust in you.

Allow the quality to reverberate from inside you to your surroundings as you invoke it.

In the case of loving-kindness, you can see not just your loved ones, but also those you don't usually care for in real life. With practice, you might even be able to aim it at people you dislike. The goal is to transcend your biases and train yourself to be capable of shutting off prejudice and seeing beyond it.

Continue to extend the quality feel to all beings in the universe. Imagine it flowing from your heart to them.

You should practice this form of meditation regularly so that the Four Divine Abodes become second nature to you. Adopting these characteristics will allow you to see the true nature of life. This encourages you to be more confident. It assists you in and your mindfulness and energy levels so that the energy you give off is optimistic and makes those around you see joy and happiness in their own lives.

The Six Perfections

The Six Perfections (paramita) consisted of the path of the Bodhisattva. It was designed to combine compassion with discernment into the true essence of life. They are:

- Generosity,
- Moral behavior,
- Patience,
- Effort,
- Concentration, and
- Wisdom.

Let us take a look at the practical steps you can take to instill the Six Perfections in your life:

Generosity

To be generous means to be open to helping others without expecting anything in return. There are several ways to become more generous to others, but in traditional Buddhist teachings, there are four ways:

To Share the Teachings of the Buddha

It is a charitable act to guide others down a path that will liberate them from their misery. It encourages others to think and act for themselves and obtain the inspiration needed to live a more meaningful life. This isn't as difficult as you would imagine. When you feel the positivity of your belief in Buddhist philosophy, you will pass it on to others and share the joy that it brings to your life. Each individual must forge their own path in life. You cannot make the decision for them. You should, however, influence those you care for to learn the kind of spirit that comes with knowing you. Give without expecting anything in return. When you do this, you feel closer to spiritual awakening than when you add strings to the gifts you offer.

To Protect Other Beings

Every day, other living creatures, including humans and animals, face life-threatening situations. The only way for them to be rescued is with others' assistance in better roles than they are. You should give up your time and energy to help protect them and lead them to a better life. This could mean donating to the needy or being generous with your time while people are sick and lonely in everyday life. There are several ways to provide security to others, and it's likely that you already do so for your relatives. Extend your safety to those in your immediate vicinity who are less fortunate than you.

To Inspire and Motivate Others

One of the best ways you can help others is by motivating them to have the courage to pursue a better life. You can also practice what you teach through meditation and follow the teachings of the Buddha. When others see that you are capable of it, they might be inspired to do the same. Inspiration does not involve any expectations. You can share what you know and discuss Buddhism's teachings, but you cannot influence people to follow the way simply because you say so. They need to see your example and to be inspired by it, rather than being expected to follow a way that does not seem natural to them.

Offering Material Goods

To improve their quality of life, living beings need food, shelter, clothes, and other resources. Your generosity in the form of such gifts would be extremely beneficial to them. In fact, this approach is most closely aligned with the idea of kindness. People offer alms in the Protestant and Catholic religions. There are money collections used for the good of the church or other individuals. There are still those who have less than you when you have things you no longer need. Offering them the things you know would make their lives easier should become a natural progression for those who follow Buddhist philosophy.

Moral Behavior

Moral behavior is exercising self-discipline so that you do not cause harm to other beings. The effort placed into choosing the more difficult but morally upright path instead of the easy but wrong one is one way to uphold this Perfection. Another is to cultivate genuine compassion for others through prayer, meditation, and good work.

Through constant practice, moral behavior will become more natural and spontaneous to you.

Patience

The more you practice the teachings of the Buddha, the more naturally patient you will be. Being patient actually protects yourself and others because it restrains you from allowing feelings, such as ill will and anger to transform into destructive actions. As your patience continues to grow, you will notice that such negative feelings become weaker until you can no longer feel them.

To help you develop patience, here are traditional Buddhist practices to try:

Acknowledge and Accept Suffering

Life is peppered with positive and negative experiences, making suffering an inevitable part of life. However, by accepting this reality, you develop the patience to go through these negative experiences. Through this, you do not become overwhelmed by feelings of regret, resentment, or anger associated with these events in your life. The acceptance of the Four Noble Truths will help you with this. The very first Noble Truth tells you that suffering is something that happens in life. However, when you strengthen your ability to accept suffering, you are stronger when such an event causes suffering.

Stay Calm

Staying calm despite frustrating or dangerous events actually leads to good karmic results. At first, it might be a challenge to stay calm when someone is attacking you. However, by taking a step back, you can analyze the best steps you can take based on the situation before you react. The more you practice, the easier it will be for you to stay calm and be mindful before speaking, acting, or even reacting.

Develop Patience in Pursuit

As you continue to practice the Buddha's teachings, there will be times when your old habits resurface and tempt you to steer from the path. However, you must remain patient in your efforts even if you do not always see immediate results. To do that, simply draw yourself back by reminding yourself of the teachings that have led you to start your journey in the first place. You will find that meditation and mindfulness will help you with your patience levels. You will be less inclined to make hasty decisions and thus be more capable of looking at problems from a global scale than the narrow focus that small-mindedness encourages. Since you are naturally more generous with people, you will find you are naturally more generous with your time and understanding.

Effort

The effort, in this sense, refers to one's commitment and perseverance in choosing to do what is right. It also means doing things with enthusiasm instead of feeling as if you are abstaining and resisting something. Some Buddhist teachers even emphasize that effort is the foundation of the other Perfections because, with it, the rest would naturally fall into place.

To practice Effort, you must understand and acknowledge the presence of the three obstacles that impede it. These are defeatism, trivial pursuits, and laziness.

Defeatism is entertaining negative, self-defeating thoughts, such as thinking that you do not have what it takes or letting your fears overcome you. You can overcome this through mantras or affirmations that remind you that you can be committed and perseverant if you so try.

Trivial pursuits are the activities that distract you and keep you from achieving your full potential. They serve no meaningful purpose in your life other than to grant you momentary and superficial desires. While there is nothing wrong with relaxing and engaging in them occasionally, you should work against becoming addicted to them.

Laziness is simply choosing not to do something because you do not want to. You can think of it as a merger between the first two obstacles because your negative mindset towards the task causes you to engage in trivial pursuits instead - a common phenomenon known as procrastination.

The only way to get out of it is by having the energy to just do the task right away. Of course, it would be easier to do that if you equip yourself with good physical and mental health and apply the right strategies, such as starting the morning right.

Concentration

Meditation is important for improving focus, so make time to practice it every day. Begin with easy meditation exercises, including sitting and breathing meditation. After you've gotten used to them, you can progress to deeper levels, such as those that enable you to minimize physical pain and emotional distress. Sit and meditate, take a sitting position on a cushion on the floor with your legs bent at the knees, and cross at the ankles. It is difficult for people who are new to meditation to adopt the more conventional lotus pose initially, but this position is ideal for meditation if your back is straight. Cup your hands with your palms facing up and your thumbs touching. If you use a pillow for meditation, sway from left to right and back again to ensure your body is grounded and secure before beginning the breathing exercises. When you begin to meditate, make sure you are in a quiet place free of distractions.

To aid the operation, close your eyes. Then, take a deep breath in through your nostrils until you feel the air filling your upper gut. Consider the air entering your body. Many Buddhists initially use a counting system but later discover that they no longer need it because their bodies have become accustomed to the rhythm of breathing and no longer need the count. The optimal count for inhalation is 8 and for exhalation is 2. The only thoughts you can have when meditating are those of the present moment and the act of breathing. Detach yourself from the world and your problems, and as thoughts arise, learn to let them go because this is not the time, but don't overthink it because it is normal for the mind to process thoughts.

Early morning meditation will improve your concentration levels during the day, allowing you to have more energy to deal with the challenges that life throws at you. Meditation is a normal event that should be as natural to you as breathing.

Wisdom

Wisdom, the highest degree of Perfections, is the ability to discern one's own thoughts to choose what is best for the good of others and oneself. The Perfection of Wisdom, according to Buddhism, is the ability to see truth as it is without being clouded by your own judgments.

As always, the only advice to follow to cultivate Wisdom is to follow the Buddha's teachings. If you want to know where to start, you can start by identifying your habitual thinking patterns. One critical thinking pattern to recognize is how you usually perceive yourself, other people, and your surroundings. Then, if you find that your emotions, words, and behavior are being driven by your own misguided perceptions, you should take action.

You might be wondering how you can discover the nature of life and enlightenment by service to others, the Four Divine Abodes, and the Six Perfections. The only way to find out is to get out there and practice them. After that, you should think about answering those questions again.

Keeping a diary at the end of and day's meditation allows you to track your progress. In reality, it also serves another function. When you finish meditating, your heart rate will be slower, and your blood pressure will be lower. Keeping a journal of your progress and ideas about what you can do the next time you meditate to help the process gives your body time to return to the normal heartbeat and blood pressure before rising to begin your day. Consider it the record of your success in your meditation and concentration practice.

Chapter 10: Exploring the Treasures and Poisons of Buddhism

The Three Treasures, also known as the "Three Jewels," are the cornerstones of Buddhism. They are the Buddha, the Dharma, and the Sangha. When aspirants seek to become Buddhists, which is by accepting the teachings and seeking to practice them, traditionally they would declare the following:

"I take refuge in the Buddha, I take refuge in the Dharma, I take refuge in the Sangha."

In other words, whenever they find themselves lost amid the mundane world, they can always find their way back with the help of the Three Treasures. Now, let us take a look at each of the Three Treasures:

The Buddha

The Buddha is the first of the Three Treasures. Take care not to interpret the meaning of the phrase "I take refuge in the Buddha" as seeking the protection and benevolence of a god. Rather, it means that you are opening your mind to the path that will lead you to become a Buddha.

Taking refuge in the Buddha means acknowledging the possibility of becoming like Buddha and being instilled with the mindset that can lead to Enlightenment attainment. The Buddha that you see on the altar of Buddhist Temples is not a god. He is an inspiration for all those who seek to become Buddhas themselves. Nowadays, there are many representations of Buddha in the western world that you can use yourself in your meditation space to help you be inspired when you step into your practice of mindfulness and meditation.

The Dharma

The Second Treasure is Dharma, and it is the teachings of the Buddha. The Four Noble Truths serve as the foundation of this Treasure. By "taking refuge in the Dharma," you acknowledge the value of learning the Four Noble Truths and practicing the Noble Eightfold Path. It's a good idea to regularly read the Noble Eightfold Path's text and keep this in short-form note format. You are easily reminded of what is expected of you when you follow the route created for your sense of happiness by the original Buddha.

The Sangha

The Sangha is a community of Buddhists. In the traditional Theravada teachings, it is composed only of the monastery. However, among Mahayanists and Buddhist modernists, it encompasses all who follow the same path, pointed by the Buddha. A Buddhist can find and give guidance to fellow Buddhists by coming together to learn and practice. The Buddha recognizes the value of interacting with those on the same path. Therefore, the Sangha is recognized as the Third Treasure. If you want to seek the guidance of those who are already Buddhas, then a temple may be able to give you this guidance. Similarly, a guru may be able to answer questions that you may have about the teachings. There are Buddhist centers worldwide that serve as communities for those seeking out the original Buddha's teachings.

Now that you know of the Three Treasures, would you agree that finding refuge in them enables you to stay on the path towards Enlightenment? Only you can tell, for your experiences are always the best testament to this tenet.

Next, we have to look at the Poisons of Buddhism, or "The Three Fires Of Buddhism".

These three are often considered as the inner character flaws that are present in all sentient beings.

Moha or Delusion

The Buddhist concept of *moha* can be translated to delusion, dullness, or confusion. A being's ignorance can be traced to this root. According to traditional Mahayanists, it is the reason for a being's destructive thoughts and actions. In the Wheel of Life, moha is represented by the boar.

The cure for Moha *lies* in Wisdom or *prajna*.

Raga or Greed

The Sanskrit word *raga* literally translates to "color" or "hue," but it represents the qualities of greed, lust, desire, and sensual attachment. All forms of craving, particularly those sensual and sexual in nature, fall under this poison. Any being who seeks and finds excitement over worldly pleasures that can be felt by the senses is afflicted by it. The rooster is the symbol for raga in the Wheel of life.

The cure for Raga can be found in Generosity or *dana*.

Dvesha or Ill Will

The term *dveshais* Sanskrit and means "hate" or "aversion." It is represented by the snake in the Wheel of Life. Harboring dvesha towards anything, including other beings and yourself, leads to suffering.

One can be cured of Dvesha through loving-kindness or metta.

If you take a look at an image of the Wheel of Life, you will see at the center the Three Poisons as their animal representations. Specifically, you will notice that the snake and the rooster are coming out from the mouth of the boar. This means that the first poison — delusion — is the source of the latter two poisons — greed and ill will.

However, what is a delusion? It is the mindset attached to a false sense of self and reality. To help you recognize the presence of the first poison, here is a famous Buddhist story:

Close your eyes and visualize that you are outside walking in the evening, lamp in hand. The moon is hidden in the clouds, but the stars are out and are enough to guide you as you follow the path that is familiar to you. Then, ahead of you, you see something.

It is long and coiled, and it appears as if it is ready to strike out at you. You feel a sense of panic as your body is suddenly frozen with fear. Then, the clouds moved, allowing the moonlight to shine on this coil, and you realized...it is merely a piece of rope.

Just to be on the safe side, though, you decide to move your lamp around you to check whether there really is a snake around. After doing so, you realize that there was no snake in the area in the first place. It was just the idea of the possibility that struck you. Your mind relaxes, and your heart drops back to its normal rate as you continue to follow the path.

After reading this analogy, what do you think the "snake" represents? If you think that it represents your false sense of self, then you are right. But as long as you hold on to the idea that that piece of rope was a snake, then you will continue to feel fear, stress, sadness, disappointment — suffering. However, through wisdom as symbolized by the moonlight, and if you make an effort to look around, you will discover that this false sense of self does not really exist.

Therefore, the Three Poisons cure acknowledges that your concept of who you are or should be is false. Once you let go of this, you can move towards cultivating wisdom, generosity, and loving kindness.

Chapter 11: The Art of Practicing Buddhism in Day-to-Day Life

The Benefits of Practicing Buddhism in Everyday Life

Before I share the techniques as to how you can incorporate Buddhism in your day-to-day life, I believe it is essential to understand the four primary benefits of practicing Buddhism.

The Psychological Benefits of Practicing Buddhism

Buddhism is primarily concerned with cognition, sensations, emotions, and feelings; thus, Buddhism recognizes emotional and cognitive causes of suffering. By the enlightenment, one comes to the realization of the impermanence of suffering. The recognition that all experience is preceded by the mind, made by the mind, and led by the mind, brings you to the ultimate realization that you are the cause of your suffering. This bonds well with the common adage that experience and success have not so much to do with what really happens to you, but so much to do with how you respond to what happens to you.

The Mental Benefits of Practicing Buddhism

Clinical psychiatrists have alluded to how your negative mind perceptions can lead to various mental illnesses, including stress, anxiety, depression, delusion, and many other serious forms of mental disorders. Practicing Buddhism purifies your mind from these wrong perceptions and thus enables you to have peace and serenity.

The Physical Benefits of Practicing Buddhism

Many clinical psychiatrists have proven negative mind perceptions as one of the leading causes of emotional distress. They have also shown how emotional distress can cause various physical illnesses such as ulcers, hypertension, and cardiovascular arrest. Purification of your mind through practicing Buddhism ensures that you detoxify your mind from triggering dangerous emotional affliction.

As you have journeyed through this book, you have consumed a lot of information about Buddhism. You are likely a bit overwhelmed right now — there really is a lot to take in. In fact, this book only barely touches the top of all of the teachings of the Buddha. However, you are likely to have a general understanding of some of the most important aspects of Buddhism by now. The next question is to determine if you want to bring Buddhism into your life. If you want to learn more about Buddhism, there is plenty of information and resources available to teach you. If you have read this book and decided that you would like to give Buddhism a try, you must still continue learning. This book is merely a guide for a beginner. In no way does this book encompass all that is Buddhism.

With that said, as you start your journey down the path to enlightenment, you may wonder how you actually get started on bringing Buddhism into your daily life. No, you do not have to start wearing robes, and no, you do not have to join a monastery. There are no secret clubs to join, no Buddhist secrets to keep. The journey to enlightenment is just that — a journey. It has to start somewhere, so why not start with the first step? Here will discover some easy ways that you can start to incorporate Buddhism into your everyday life.

The Spiritual Benefits of Practicing Buddhism

The highest aspiration of those who seek spirituality is to be in a state of perfect harmony with the nature of one's own being, nature of other beings, and nature of things. In this state of perfect harmony, peace abounds as there are no conflicts but right knowledge and right understanding. These are the highest aspirations that those who belong to religions do seek to achieve.

Negative conflicts, violence, and wars are all attributed to ignorance and selfish desires. These selfish desires can only be conquered by compassion and wisdom, and you can only achieve absolute compassion through enlightenment; thus, by gaining enlightenment, one can overcome all forms of illnesses, negative conflicts, violence, and wars. Knowledge can bring liberation to the entirety of humankind and bring humanity to a state of perpetual joy, peace, serenity, and harmony. This state is known as nirvana.

Practicing Buddhism

The best way to start practicing Buddhism is to find a Buddhist center. Here, you will be given much more in-depth information about the teachings of the Buddha. These centers are made for beginners and established Buddhists. The atmosphere will be welcoming because, well, that is the way of the Buddhist — love, kindness, and compassion. There will be plenty of written information you can take home with you to study on your own. There will also be Buddhist teachers who will assist you in understanding all of the teachings. You will learn how to meditate, an essential aspect of Buddhism. The reason that it is always best to seek out a practiced Buddhist for teachings is that there is only so much information and understanding you can take from books and articles. Having a teacher discuss your studies can be a great tool for traveling down your path to enlightenment with more ease.

As you begin your path to enlightenment, you need to learn all that you can about Buddhism. There are different paths to enlightenment, so you must study each one to find the path that fits your life the best. Buddhism's different paths usually have the same basic ideas but incorporate their own understandings of the Buddha's teachings into the path. So, you will find variances between the paths. There are thousands of books available to teach you about Buddhism. It is important to focus on one aspect at a time. If you try to cram in all of the Buddha's teachings as fast as you can, you will never understand what you are learning. You will also likely just get overwhelmed and fed up, leading you to give up on Buddhism.

A Buddhist teacher can help you with so many questions and aspects of Buddhism to make the best choice for you. A teacher can also monitor your readings and studying so that you stay focused without getting overwhelmed. However, not everyone has immediate access to a Buddhist center, so you may need to take the first steps on your own. Choose a specific aspect of Buddhism to study and learn. You want to absorb absolutely all of the knowledge of the aspect until you have a complete understanding. Only then should you move on to another aspect. Take your time with your studies. Utilize the internet to find other Buddhists online who will answer your questions and help guide you on your path.

You can start off slow, just simply learning some basic Buddhist terminology. You can start at the beginning and delve deep into the Buddha's story and Buddhism's origins. The goal is to choose a place to start, stick with it until you really understand it, and then move on to another area of study. You can study as much or as little as you feel comfortable doing. Some people want to immerse themselves in Buddhism from the beginning — they are just that excited to go down the Path of Enlightenment. However, others choose to take a more cautious journey, taking their time with the teachings, asking all of the hard questions, and gaining as much insight as possible before taking even one more step. You decide how you want to learn about Buddhism — you are the only one who knows what is best for you.

Community is a crucial part of Buddhism. Buddhists need each other to learn from and to help guide. You need a strong, smart support system during your path to nirvana. You cannot learn all that you need to learn alone. If there is not a

Buddhist center near your location, then take it to the internet. There are plenty of Buddhist forums, groups, websites, etc., that are full of practicing Buddhists who will provide you with the encouraging support system you need. They will also give you a place to take your questions, your anxieties, your concerns and learn how to release all of them. Online groups can even help you with meditation.

One way you can bring Buddhism into your everyday life is to just take the time to sit every day. Sitting in peace and quiet is your first step towards mindful meditation. If you cannot sit still for a few minutes each day, completely still, then you have to keep practicing. Meditation requires a stillness of the body and the mind, so start off with just sitting quietly. You do not necessarily have to worry about clearing your mind yet. You just want to ensure you can sit still for a bit of time. Start with five minutes each day. As you become more comfortable with just sitting in peace, add more time to each session. Eventually, you can start to bring meditation into the session.

Since Buddhism is a way of living your life, you have to be prepared to make many changes, especially in your awareness and understanding of the world around you and your own mind. Awareness is a key point of Buddhism, so learning a proper meditation method is ideal. You must be able to clear your mind to attain a level of purity in your mind that will lead you to enlightenment. You can practice meditation at home, on your own, with information you learn about meditation. You can practice meditation in a group setting with other blossoming Buddhists. You will likely find online groups where you can meditate "virtually" with a group. As long as you learn how to meditate, and you go further and further with each session into reaching that supreme level of a pure mind, then you are on the right track to enlightenment.

To bring Buddhism into your everyday life other than studying and meditation, just start living a kind and compassionate life. You want to put forth positive, happy energy in everything you do because, as you know, karma is watching. So, live your life knowing that karma will always find you. You are going to struggle during your Buddhism journey. There will be negative times as you learn more and more about the true nature of reality. You will likely have to face some hard truths about yourself and how you live or feel. Just keep going forward. You are not going to become a fully-fledged, enlightened Buddhist in just a few weeks or months. You are looking at years of studying and practicing and changing and living your new life before reaching nirvana.

While this probably sounds overwhelming, it will be worth the effort and the wait. Once you reach the enlightenment level, you will no longer struggle with letting go of clinging, accepting that all things change, living a simple life, and with total awareness. You will be awakened — you will be like the Buddha. You will have a full understanding of your mind, your life, and your actions, as well as your feelings and thoughts. You will be a Buddhist, and your future will be very bright.

Setting Up Your Homespace For Meditation

For those who live in areas where Buddhist temples are prevalent, creating a personal meditation space is not as important. However, for those in the Western world where finding a temple can be nearly impossible, having a place in your home to practice is vital. Even if you choose not to subscribe fully to the Path of Enlightenment, meditation can have an enormous effect on everything in your life. Through meditation, you learn to control your mind, dig deeper into your unconscious mind, and soothe your body from the anxiety-ridden world outside your doors.

There are many different things to run over before creating your meditation space. You don't want to just plop a pillow in the middle of the living room and attempt to find inner meditative calmness, especially for those who don't live alone. Your space should be sacred to you and only used when looking for deep meditation. It doesn't have to be its own room, but it should be a space that is left undisturbed by others. By understanding what you need to create this sacred space, you will be able to do so wherever you go, whether in your home, a friend's home, or in a hotel when away for vacation or business. The following section will look at the things you should look at when creating your meditation space.

Keeping Your Intentions in Check

Not everybody who builds a meditation space intends to fully immerse themselves in the life of a Buddhist. In reality, some people just want a quiet place to sit and focus on the present. Your meditation and reflection room will be tailored to your unique requirements, so take the time to consider your goals. If they are for deep meditation, it is important to choose a location in your home where you can find peace and quiet. You might also discover that being near to nature aids you in your search. As a result, if you have a garden area where you can get away from the hustle and bustle of life, this would be a good place for your meditation.

Whatever the reason for your desire for a meditation room, recognize and understand that the daily world is filled with obstacles to practicing mindfulness and awareness. There are inventions all around us that prevent our true selves from getting the care and exercise they need to become aware of the reality around them, such as television, computers, and even your phone. Understanding your intentions will assist you in determining precisely what sort of room you will need.

Finding the Right Space

When you know your intentions, you'll know what kind of room you're looking for in your home. You don't need to devote an entire room to meditation, but if that is feasible for you, go for it! A corner of a room, on the other hand, where you know the activities of that space perfectly match your intentions, is exactly what you're looking for. Remember to find a room that will not be disrupted by the acts, objects, or pets in your home when it is not in use. Nothing is more annoying when you sit in stillness than cat fur rising up from your meditation pillow.

For those with more experience in the art of meditation, consider an outdoor room that can be used in any weather condition. For example, since we have three dogs and a child in our house, my meditation space is under the deck's covered part in front of my Buddha statue. Since I live in the mountains, I designate a place in my bedroom as a meditation area during the cold winters. Your meditation room should be tailored to your specific needs. One friend who meditates regularly has chosen a location in the open, high in the hills, where she can get close to nature and experience the oneness she feels is part of her sanctity. Her reasoning can be helpful to those who find themselves in similar situations. When you're in a place that really inspires you, you realize how tiny you are, and that's just the beginning. Being small and modest is an integral part of Buddhism, and you often believe that the world around you encourages you to be the best that you can be, no matter how small nature makes you feel. Being tiny is not a bad thing. Every pebble on the beach has a specific location.

This is a very personal decision based on what really relaxes you. The sounds of nature and the warmth of the sun are where I feel the calmest, but you may live in a city where the honking of horns and the sounds of people can be extremely distracting. Buddhist temples can be found in every aspect of society, from serene mountain tops to city strip malls. The argument is that when you step through those doors and into that room, you find a sense of peace that is detached from the noise of the world around you.

Fixing the Decor

This is your personal space, and you can decorate it in any manner you wish. Most take a minimalistic approach to avoid distractions, but you can decorate your area in any way you want. Think about the things that bring you the most comfort and relaxation and incorporate them into your space. If you are uncomfortable, your mind will be uncomfortable as well, and you will find that reaching a deep stillness and meditative state will be difficult. Just as finding intentions and deciding upon a space, decorating your meditation area is a hugely personal decision.

My meditation space outside is simply my Buddha statue and my meditation pillow. The outside nature brings all the decor I need to feel at peace. HOWEVER, when I bring it inside, it takes a bit more effort to separate the comfort of my home from the pure comfort of a place of peace. I use soft blankets to help calm me, a Buddha picture because the statue is too large to bring indoors, candles for a calming sense, and incense in a fragrance that invokes spiritual ideas. Your decor may also align with any Buddhist rituals you may decide upon. Often, your space may change if you observe any holidays associated with Buddhism.

Different things give inspiration to different people. You may find that you have a particular photograph that is inspirational, and that's something that you can incorporate into your meditation space as well because sometimes the type of meditation can be focused meditation which means that you meditate with your eyes open but concentrate on a particular object that you find to be inspirational.

However you decide to decorate your space, make sure that it is comforting, safe, and right for you. This, as you can see, is a common theme in Buddhism since the path to Enlightenment, though often reached through the same routines, is an extremely personal journey that you take.

Remember that becoming comfortable in this life is important because even if you achieve true Enlightenment, you still have to live in this life.

The Theme

The path you face will influence your meditative state's outcome depending on the type of meditation you practice. Consider your meditation requirements when selecting a location and selecting a decor. Remember that whatever you feel before closing your eyes will help your mind relax and allow you to connect with your inner self. Those who prefer a more calming and relaxing meditation often face north, while those who prefer a more rejuvenating meditation face east or west. These variations are determined by the type of Buddhism you practice, as well as your intention for stillness. When I design my interior room, I try to make it as relaxing as possible so that even if I turn my pillow away from my focal point, I am still comfortable and at ease. My bedroom, for example, is very simply furnished, and before I begin my meditation, I make certain that everything is picked up and somewhat organized. Clutter can trigger anxiety, which stimulates my conscious mind and prevents me from being still.

Items You May Want for Your Space

As mentioned before, your space is a reflection of your own personal comfort and intention. You may have an incredibly spiritual area, while you may also have a simple space not related to religious or spiritual ideas. These are some of the pieces that you may find useful in your newly-created meditation space.

Buddha

Because religion is such a pertinent thing in society, we often think of statues or pictures as worshipping items. However, as we have said before, there is no ultimate creator that we focus on in Buddhism. Buddha is a teacher and a symbol of mindfulness and intention. Having a visual representation of Enlightenment and the wise teachings of the first Buddha may help you focus, be reminded of mindfulness, and remember the teachings that these individuals gave to help you on your path to Enlightenment.

Candles and Incense

Candles are among my favorite comfort things to have in my home. Bright artificial lights always stiffen my resolve to let go and let my inner self take over. However, total darkness makes me tired, and in such a hectic world, meditation can often push me to sleep. Candles help me concentrate my mind. They provide an excellent focal point for me, and the shadows they cast to aid in releasing stress from my physical body. Personally, I prefer unscented candles because scented candles are always too artificial for me, but you can choose any kind, color, and size of candle you like. Just make sure they're in a safe position, so you don't have to worry about them when trying to meditate. A curtain fire will break you out of your meditative state faster than anything else.

Incense is not for all, but I've always used it to help me relax. Lavender is my favorite incense fragrance because it calms my nerves and brings peace to my space. Incense often lingers for a long time, so even when I'm not meditating and walking by my bed, I catch a whiff of lavender and am immediately reminded to remember my intentions for the day and be aware of the world around me. When burning incense, make sure to keep it in a safe position and avoid putting it directly in front of you. The smoke from it can be powerful, but if it is burning on the other side of the building, you will get a passing scent to help you get your thoughts back on track.

Meditation Pillow

One of the most irritating and distracting aspects of meditation is ignoring the pain the body wants to distract you from. Let's face it, sitting for hours on the floor might have been comfortable when we were ten years old, but as we get older, it isn't always the best option. There are so many things that can distract you, from aching backs to numbness in your limbs. Meditation pillows, especially those designed specifically for meditation, help align your body with the proper posture and keep it relaxed during the process.

My personal meditation pillow selection involves a big flat pillow and a small bean-filled pillow under my buttocks. The wide pillow prevents my knees from being sore when lying on the ground, while the one for sitting conforms to my body in such a way that I can sit cross-legged and at an angle. This keeps my back and neck aligned and prevents aching spots when I'm trying to concentrate. In fact, all you really need is your body and a place to sit, and while I've trained myself to be able to meditate anywhere, particularly because I travel so frequently, I want to make sure I'm as distraction-free as possible at home.

There is nothing wrong with having a hard chair for those unable to sit on a cushion on the floor. The location for meditation on a chair would be slightly different in that you would center your body during meditation by placing your feet flat on the floor. As a result, you need a chair with a straight back rather than one that allows you to recline. The chair's height should be such that your feet can be laid flat on the floor without difficulties.

Singing Bowl

Singing bowls are used for various things, from meditation and music to rituals and funerals. The singing bowl produces a soothing and calm sound that can help your mind relax into a meditative state. Often, they are used to signal the beginning and end of a meditation. You can ring a singing bowl and then start your breathing, falling further into meditation and finding that you don't even hear the sound anymore. Sometimes they can be used simply to realign you and bring calming energy. A singing bowl of the right pitch can also be used to start your chant. This is a good way to start your meditation session if you use chant, but remember that chanting takes some practice.

Ring the singing bowl and then breathe in. On the outward breath, you tend to sing the Om or your chosen chant and then breathe in again. You may find during meditation that you no longer need the chant, but if this is your way of meditating and you are more comfortable with it, the bowl should be placed near to your place of meditation so that after the initial sound from the bowl, the bowl is replaced beside you as you continue your journey into meditation.

The further you delve into your meditation routine, the more you will be aware of what you need in your space to make it the perfect tranquil location. Nature is everywhere and in everything, so if your space is inside, inviting pieces of nature, such as rocks and plants into your space, may help to align you. Soft colors, soft music, and temperature control are also important things to think about when entering your space. Once you know what will work for you in your complete space, you will be able to move and bend with that to create spaces in other places, such as your office, a hotel room, and even when you are on vacation. The most important aspect of all of this is to feel comfortable and intentional in your actions and enjoy everything around you.

Eventually, you will find that all of that comfort comes from within you and that you can meditate in any space and not be put off by your surroundings. If you want to try something really special that is comforting and wonderfully calming, then I would advise that you choose a spot where you can see a lot of the natural environment and enjoy the warmth of the sunset or sunrise, combining your meditation with yoga practices that help you to feel the balance of the world around you, within you.

Chapter 12: Understanding How Yoga can Bring Peace to Your Mind

Where Does Yoga Originate From?

It is said that yoga originated in pre-Vedic (3300 BCE) India, as some Indus Valley seals depict human figures performing what looks like common yoga or meditation poses, such as the headstand. However, these interpretations are considered uncertain and inconclusive.

Traditional Hinduism regards the Vedas (a large body of knowledge texts from ancient India) as the ultimate spiritual knowledge source. These texts describe several ascetic practices (which include meditation and the use of bodily poses), and many scholars believe that they *might* have been precursors to yoga.

The characteristic elements of yoga were practiced, but no direct evidence of it being "yoga" exists.

A textual reference to yoga began to emerge in texts dating from 500-200 BCE. The first appearance of the term with the same meaning is found in the *Katha Upanishad*. The scriptures define yoga as "the steady control of the senses." Along with conscious control of our mental activity, it leads to a supreme state.

This connects with the modern definition of yoga as a process of interiorization and ascension.

The classical era (200 BCE-500 CE) saw many texts that systematically compiled several yoga methods and practices.

Hatha yoga specifically surfaced during the Middle Ages (500-1500 CE). This period displayed several improvements and refinements to the traditions of yoga.

One of the first references to Hatha yoga can be found in Buddhist texts from the 8th century. However, the earliest full definition is found in the 11th-century Buddhist text *Vimalaprabha*. It refined the bodily poses (asanas) into the full range of body poses that are popular today. The 15th century CE saw the birth of the HathapradipiK, one of the most influential compilations of Hatha yoga. It included information about the six acts of body cleansing, the asanas, pranayama, meditation, and other topics.

Thanks to the open nature of Hatha yoga, which did not limit its practices to persons of a specific sex, caste, class, or creed, it quickly became a broader movement.

A word about the traditional goal of Hatha yoga. The original objective of Hatha yoga was to attain physical *siddhis* (read as special powers or characteristics such as slowed aging) as well as "liberation" *(moksha)*. These *siddhis* are more symbolic than anything else, merely reflecting the soteriological desires of Indian religions.

What Exactly is Yoga?

Broadly speaking, yoga refers to a collection of practices for the body, mind, and soul which originated in ancient India. Etymologically, yoga stems from the Sanskrit root yuj, which means "to add" or "to unite."

Essentially, yoga is more than physical exercise. It is a meditative practice with a spiritual core. Through its practice, yogis seek to reach the moksha, liberation." This liberation refers to "breaking out" of the cycle of death and rebirth. It means liberating ourselves from ignorance.

The precise definition of the term "yoga" varies with the context, but most of the time, it refers to:

- A disciplined method of achieving a goal
- A set of techniques to control both mind and body
- A school of philosophy

The Practice of Yoga

Yoga involves static principles that vary slightly from one school to another while maintaining the same ultimate purpose: liberation.

This refers to yoga as a means of discovering the dysfunctions in our perception and cognition. Through yoga, we overcome these to liberate ourselves from suffering, bringing forth inner peace and salvation.

By meditating with yoga, we raise and expand our consciousness. We change the lens to become coextensively aware of all that surrounds us and not just ourselves.

Yogis must carve a path to omniscience and heightened consciousness with yoga. The end goal is breaking our chains to falsehood and suffering. We are meant to understand both the impermanent and permanent realities that clash in life.

Please note that if you are pregnant, nursing, have sustained injuries, or have any other condition that might conflict with you practicing yoga, it's important to consult the appropriate health services first before starting with yoga.

The Different Schools of Yoga

It is important to understand that *all* yoga schools stem from "classical yoga," which is considered one of the *astika* (Sanskrit word for "there it is" or "exists") schools of Hinduism.

In effect, yoga refers to various schools with their own practices, methods, and philosophies extending to different Jain, Buddhist, and Hindu practices.

We can find Jnana yoga, Karma yoga, Bhakti yoga, and Hatha yoga among these Hindu schools.

Hatha yoga ("Hatha" being the Sanskrit word for "force") focuses on exercises to cultivate strength, both physical and mental. The exercises in question are none other than the poses adopted in yoga, called *asanas* (the Sanskrit word for "sitting down" or "to sit down").

For this reason, this book will focus on Hatha yoga. While other yoga schools *do* have asanas, Hatha yoga is *focused* on mastering the body through them. Hatha yoga is about using diet to purify our body, *pranayama* (breathing techniques) to master our life energy, and asanas to master our physical abilities, obtaining the *siddhis* (special body powers) in the process.

Traditionally speaking, there are a few rules for performing the asanas:

- Asanas *should* be performed while fasting.
- Force *should not* be applied. The body *should not* tremble.
- The parts of the body *should* be moved slowly, particularly the head and heels.
- The breathing *should* be controlled (referred to as *"pranayama",* the Sanskrit word for "breath control" or "control of the breath" - more about it later).
- Stress from the body *should* be released with special poses *before* performing other asanas.

Following these traditional rules, while not mandatory, can be very helpful for any prospective yogi.

It would be wise to remember that practicing yoga should be comfortable regardless of your skill level. You shouldn't push your body into discomfort at any point. Try your best *not to* turn yoga into a competition with yourself.

The goal here is to master your body. Beginners won't feel too comfortable; it will take several short sessions with relatively simple poses. As the yogi advances, he or she becomes unattached from the feeling of discomfort.

This is vital to reach the spiritual goal of yoga, which is detachment from suffering.

Besides the asanas, Hatha yoga extends to other practices. The philosophy behind it states that a successful yogi should display the following characteristics:

- *Utsaha* ("enthusiasm" or "fortitude")
- *Sahasa* ("courage" or "optimism") *Dhairya* (*"patience"* or "persistence")
- *Jnana Tattva* ("knowledge")
- *Nishcaya* ("resolve" or "determination")
- *Tyaga* ("solitude" or "renunciation")

It's easy for westerners to assume that Hatha yoga (or even yoga in general) is *exclusively* about asanas.

Despite this mistaken conception, Hatha yoga encompasses more than that. It blends different ideas, such as ethics, diet, cleansing, breathing and physical exercises, meditation, and spiritual development.

The Practices of a Yogi

Consequently, to be a proper yogi, one should reflect on the following practices:

"Proper" Diet

Special emphasis is given to *mitahara* (the Sanskrit word that translates to "habit of moderate food"). It consists of a heightened awareness of food, drink, diet, and consumption habits.

Ancient texts refer to *mitahara as* a concept that links proper nutrition with the body and mind's health. Some of the largest nutrition compendiums that have survived from ancient India highlight the importance of planning a diet.

The *Charaka Samhita* ("Compendium of Charaka") states that "wholesome diets promote health and growth." While coming from a collection of books from the pre-2nd century CE, this concept is in perfect accord with modern thinking.

The general idea of *mitahara* is to tailor our diet according to our body, health, climate, season, habits, and tastes and constantly rotate what we eat to avoid excesses.

Proper "Body Cleansing"

This refers to a series of practices to cleanse the body with the help of a yoga teacher. These are beyond the scope of this book; however, I will briefly list them here in case you are curious:

Neti

Yogic system for the cleaning of our air passageways. In simpler words, nasal wash with purified water and non-iodized salt.

This practice is wonderful for those who suffer nasal problems, but it should be performed with the aid of an expert and only after proper medical examination.

Dhauti

Yogic system of body cleansing techniques. This practice is directed to cleaning the digestive and respiratory tracts and the external ears and eyes.

Nauli

Yogic system for cleaning the digestive organs. It is based on the massage of the internal belly organs.

Basti

Yogic system for the cleaning of the lower abdomen. These techniques involve delicate methods and should only be practiced with the help of experts.

Kapalabhati

Yogic system for "skull polishing". In other words, a set of practices to energize the brain. Trataka Yogic meditation method. It consists of staring at a single point (generally a candle flame) for some time to "bring energy to the third eye" and to enhance our ability to concentrate.

Its purpose is to give a rest to our minds. Thus we're "cleaning" our thoughts.

"Proper" Breathing

As mentioned before, "breath control" or pranayama refers to achieving the proper way of breathing through a set of techniques to alter how we breathe.

The intention is to produce specific positive results to amplify our life force.

Several forms of pranayama exist, and they're often based on *puraka* (inhalation), *kumbhaka* (retention), and *recaka* (exhalation). Each element can get very complex, but the general idea should be enough for starters.

The Health Benefits of Yoga

Yoga offers several benefits to perseverant yogis.

Constant physical exercise, coupled with strong meditation and focus, leads to better health and well-being. This extends to the mind and the body.

You must never forget that yoga is about transcendence. A prospective yogi should seek to strengthen his body, mind, and soul. This will lead him into a path of tranquility and peace.

Let's break down the many benefits of yoga into physical and mental categories:

Physical

Yoga *is not* an aerobic exercise (except for some of the most complex poses). However, constant (as in daily) yoga exercises *will* help you build up muscle and burn calories.

For those who suffer from diabetes or other insulin-related problems, yoga allows your body to re-oxygenate at a better rate, breathing more life into your cells. In turn, this helps you regulate your blood sugar level.

Yoga poses stimulate your lymphatic system. This boosts your immune system and releases toxins from your body. Those who start practicing yoga regularly often experience a surge of energy. This can be attributed to the fact that oxygenated blood allows our bodies to perform much better.

Yoga exercise, along with controlled breathing and thoughtful meditation, can increase your overall energy. Lack of sleep, sedentary habits, and piled-up stress can lead us to feel like we're at half our potential all the time. Yoga lets you recover from that!

Yogis who practice constantly reach a point where they can push their physical boundaries far beyond what they could initially. This leads to better physical balance and more agility.

So, in a nutshell, practicing yoga will grant your body the following benefits:

- Increased flexibility and agility
- Stronger and better-toned muscles
- More energy and vitality
- Improved respiration and metabolism
- Reduced weight (closer to your ideal weight)
- Better cardiovascular and circulatory health
- Higher athletic performance

Mental

Our everyday life is full of countless stressors that make *everything* harder. As it piles on, stress takes a whole new toll on our bodies because it triggers cortisol and adrenaline release (also known as the "survival" hormones).

I'm sure that you've felt a sudden rush of energy and hastiness after a heated argument or before an important event. That's stress for you!

The surplus of "survival hormones" in our bodies serves a purpose in real survival situations, but not in our everyday life. Many of us have a hard time managing our stress levels.

Fortunately, yoga is one of the many beneficial practices that help you relax your body. With constant practice, we learn how to release muscle tension on demand, and when we get our needed dose of stretching and breathing, our body responds by triggering the release of certain "relaxation" hormones like serotonin. 20-minute yoga sessions inject more oxygen into our bloodstream, and that blood gets carried into our brain.

As we lower our stress levels, our immune system is strengthened. On the other hand, high levels of cortisol in our blood lead to a depressed immune system.

All in all, this leads to improvements in our quality of life. Better sleep is often a result of daily yoga practice.

The best part is that the mental benefits of yoga function pretty much like a positive feedback cycle. You sleep better, have less stress, and have a better outlook on life, making you sleep better!

The benefits of yoga are plentiful. You won't be lifting weights or running, but you will be cultivating your inner balance.

Some people dismiss these concepts, but the truth is that sometimes we need to take a moment to think about ourselves.

That is the primordial offer of yoga: thoughtful meditation and self-reconnection tied together with a series of poses to stretch our bodies.

So, in a nutshell, practicing yoga will grant your mind the following benefits:

- Increased focus
- Reduced stress levels
- Diminished anxiety and fidgetiness
- More motivation and willpower
- More happiness
- Heightened empathy
- Increased emotional resilience

About Pranayama

The breathing techniques of pranayama are vital for yoga, as there's an underlying link between the asanas and pranayama.

You see, in a conventional yoga class, with a yoga teacher, you're taught to *consciously* control your breathing. Many of us are accustomed *to just* breathing, period.

We don't inhale or exhale because we want to; it's just autopilot.

When practicing yoga, the efficiency of both your physical exercise and spiritual meditation can be measured by your breathing.

Breathing consciously allows you to maintain balance. It gives you more strength, endurance, and flexibility. Above everything, it gives you peace to reconnect with your inner self.

Learn the following techniques, and try to add them during your asanas:

Ocean Breath (in Sanskrit *"Ujjayi Pranayama"*). This is a classic breathing technique, perfect for relaxation and meditation

To perform it during your yoga practice: Focus solely on your breath, inhaling deeply through your nose, and then exhaling slowly, audibly making the "ah" sound. Repeat a couple of times, and then close your mouth.

Alternating Nostril Breath (in Sanskrit *"Nadi Shodhana Pranayama"*)

This therapeutic breathing technique allows you to clean and unblock your nasal cavities. To perform it during your yoga practice: Finish your asana sequence, and then prepare your mind to meditate or relax.

Bring your right hand in front of your nose, close your right nostril with your thumb, and inhale through the left nostril. Now close your left nostril with your right forefinger, open the right nostril, and exhale slowly through it. Now switch (inhale through the right nostril and exhale through the left) and complete the cycle. Repeat it from 3 to 5 times.

Breath Retention (in Sanskrit *"Kumbhaka Pranayama"*). This breathing technique lets you improve your lung capacity

To perform it during your asana practice: Finish your asana sequence, and then prepare your mind to meditate or relax.

Inhale as much as you can, filling your lungs to the max. Hold your breath for 10 seconds, and then try to inhale even more. Exhale, and wait a few seconds before trying it again. Do it 3 to 5 times.

Breath of Fire (in Sanskrit *"Kapalabhati Pranayama"*)

This rapid breathing technique is meant to give you a kick-start when you're feeling lethargic or mentally numb.

To perform it during your asana practice: Take a deep inhale, and then exhale slowly. Now, inhale again, deeply, but exhale quickly, using your lower abs to push the air out. The trick is inhaling slowly and deeply and then exhaling quickly. Repeat this process between 25 and 30 times.

Short breathing tips generally, you should:

- Exhale while bending forward
- Inhale when lifting or puffing the chest
- Exhale while you twist

Easy Yoga Poses to Know About

The bread and butter of modern yoga: The asanas!

Each pose includes its focus, the physical indications and contraindications, time to hold the pose, its Sanskrit name, and the level aimed (beginner, intermediate, or advanced).

I suggest you plan your sessions so that every two days, you switch your focus. For example, Monday and Tuesday, you work on stretching your legs, and Wednesday and Thursday, you work on stretching your arms.

Some Tips Before Beginning

Once you're done with a pose, don't rush to the next one! Transition to your new pose with calm and grace. You must invite harmony and peace to yourself when practicing yoga.

- Don't force yourself to perform complex poses. Some people mistakenly assume that they can go straight for the Firefly *(Tittibhasana)* pose just because they go to the gym every day. That is not the case! Yoga is a different beast altogether, and you need to go steady and slow.
- Don't do over 40 minutes. As you acquire more skill, you'll be met with uncomfortable

poses that will require many weeks of practice to pull off. 20 to 40-minute sessions are your best bet (I prefer the 20-minute ones). I'm referring here to the actual physical exercise. Typical yoga classes last about an hour, but they include meditation and a warm-up section. Don't extend your asana practice beyond 40 minutes.

- Count with breaths. Each pose should be held for as long as 3 to 5 deep, controlled breaths. First, you must inhale slowly, then you must hold the air, then you exhale slowly. Be sure to work on the consistency of each breath!
- Don't mix more than **20** poses. You might be eager to try a lot of poses in a single day, but generally, doing 10 to 15 a day is more than enough. If you really want to push it, **20** should be your max. Constantly practicing, improving, and lastly, mastering poses is far better for you.
- If a pose involves one side of your body, then it must be mirrored on the other side as well. So, if you stretch to the left for 3 breaths, you must stretch to the right for 3 breaths too.

The Mountain Pose (Tadasana)

"The mother of all yoga poses," says Ingber, "Mountain only appears easy." This two-footed posture serves as the basis for a variety of other positions that necessitate sensitivity and balance. "Through this pose, one seeks the correct alignment and form for additional movements," she explains.

Stand with your feet together and your arms by your sides. Be sure to drive the four corners of your feet into the dirt. Straighten your legs next, then tuck your tailbone in a while, engaging your thigh muscles. When you inhale, lengthen your torso and stretch your arms up and out. Exhale and move your shoulder blades away from your head, toward the back of your waist, as you return your arms to your sides.

Child's Pose (Balasana)

Think of this exercise as a reset button. This simple pose relaxes your nervous system and is a great place to take a breather during class if needed. If you have knee problems, take special caution when lowering into this spot.

Start in a kneeling position with your toes tucked under. Lower your buttocks to your knees while stretching your upper body forward and down with your arms extended. Your stomach should be comfortably supported by your legs, and your forehead should be in contact with the mat.

Cat/Cow Pose (Marjaryasana to Bitilasana)

Cat/cow is a perfect way to warm up your back and prepare your body for the downward-facing dog, according to Ingber. It also addresses mobility (hello desk jobs) and works your heart without the extra stress on your wrists and shoulders that a down dog step could cause.

Begin on your hands and knees on the floor, spine neutral, and abs engaged. Inhale deeply, then exhale by rounding your spine up towards the ceiling and tucking your head towards your stomach, relaxing your jaw. Arch your back and relax your abs on the next inhale. Lift your head and tailbone upwards, taking care not to strain your neck by moving too rapidly or deeply.

Downward-Facing Dog (Adho Mukha Svanansana)

Down dog, one of the most familiar poses, is a perfect way to stretch your back, elbows, arms, hamstrings, and, well, just about anything. It also helps you to feel relaxed and focused.

Get down on your hands and knees with your palms just below your shoulder and your fingers pointing upward. Your knees should be under your hips, and your toes should be tucked. Raise your hips and push your body back into a V-shape. The distance between your feet should be hip-width. Remember that it's fine if you can't get your feet to the floor (your hamstrings might be too tight). Spread your fingers and toes and move your chest to your knees.

Warrior I (Virabhadrasana I)

The first in the Warrior series, this pose strengthens your legs, while also opening your hips and chest and extending your arms and legs. While doing this exercise, you will notice an improvement in your concentration and balance, all of which are necessary for a yoga practice.

Begin in the mountain pose. When you exhale, take a four-foot step back with your left foot, putting you in a lunge stance with your right ankle over your right knee. Lift your arms above, biceps by your ears, and turn your left foot 90 degrees to face the left wall. Align your left heel parallel to your right heel. Extend your chest, draw your shoulders back, and lower yourself toward the floor while raising your arms. As you continue to breathe, keep your hips square to the front.

Warrior II (Virabhadrasana II)

Warrior II is very similar to Warrior I, except that your upper body is turned to the side instead of facing forward. Warrior II provides the same quad-strengthening advantages as Warrior I, but it also opens up your hip flexor muscles for greater flexibility.

Start in the mountain pose. Exhale and take a four-foot to step back with your left foot, making sure your heels are in line. Turn your back foot 90 degrees, so it is perpendicular to your front foot. Lift your arms to shoulder height, parallel to the floor, right arm in front, and left arm behind. Bend your front knee so that it is directly over your ankle, then sink your hips low until your front thigh is parallel to the floor. Look straight ahead with your eyes aligned with your front-facing shoulder.

Corpse Pose (Shavasana)

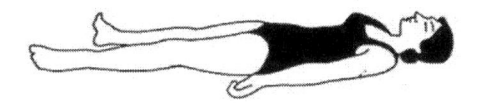

Although lying around may seem meaningless, it is one of the most meditative moments of any yoga practice. The corpse pose relaxes the body and mind by calming the mind, relieving tension, and inducing a relaxed state. (What makes you think yogis are so laid-back?)

Lie down on your back with your feet by your sides. Bring your arms opposite your torso, slightly apart, palms facing the sky. Relax your whole body, including your lips. This is usually the last pose in a lesson, and you'll stay in it for anywhere from 30 seconds to five or ten minutes. When it's time to slowly awaken your thoughts and return to a seated position, your teacher will give you a cue.

While there are hundreds and hundreds of more poses to learn, these seven should be a good starting point for you. If you find that these poses help you stay calm, then feel free to explore the art of yoga even more!

Chapter 13: Using Meditation as a Weapon Against Stress and Anxiety

How Can Meditation Help With Anxiety and Depression

You can define a healthy mind as one with no mental disorder. Mental health these days can be improved. These improvements can be made in various ways. The leading one is meditation. Meditation is both an individual and spiritual experience. Anxiety is an emotion associated with worry and tension. Everyone feels stress. Anxiety affects everyone. Here we will go through with dealing with it. Most people do not understand it. It is not just a feeling. Anxiety can never fade away. Regardless of where you are, you will always feel it. Through meditative inhalation and exhalation daily, one can improve his or her ability to deal with anxiety. Anxiety can prevent a person from working at their full potential. Stress can lead to high blood pressure. This happens when it is not maintained. It can also induce restlessness. It can also cause worry, which is uncontrollable. Anxiety can also hinder one from sleeping. Stress can lead to anger.

Meditation can help reduce anxiety - People who suffer from anxiety can overcome it. By using mindfulness meditation, one can minimize anxiety efficiently.

People think that their life is complete. No. Fear pops up. Have a huge event coming. Most of the cases of anxiety are unexpected. Meditation is the cheapest way to deal with stress. It is more effective than drugs. Its effects are long-lasting. When compared to drugs, it is more affordable and more effective. This therapy is very successful in treating depression and anxiety. These effects are long-term. The method is also less costly. Just after a few months into the program, some of the patients were already well. So, meditation works better than antidepressants to reduce anxiety. The world is full of chaos. Chaos can exert some stress on you; however, with a peaceful mind, we can deal with the disorder. Therefore, this is where peace in the brain is required.

You can eventually achieve this through meditation.

Meditation can also be used with antidepressants - Mindfulness meditation assists a lot in this sector. To reduce anxiety, one meditates by focusing on the heart. Fortunately, it boosts confidence within the meditator. With this, the more stable a person will become. One imagines that the soul is breathing. The breathing should be sincere. The person meditating should also add a feeling of appreciation. This should be practiced as frequently as possible. During this time, the meditator should think of what he or she is grateful for and highly appreciates - psychology advises people to lean on meditation to reduce anxiety. There are several types of stress. We shall highlight them. We shall look at how to deal with it through meditation.

Generalized anxiety disorder - This induces excess anxiety for an extended period. Unspecified life events cause this anxiety. It is most challenging to identify. This type of stress can be maintained. The remedy for this anxiety is also mindfulness meditation. Addition of an object to concentrate increases efficiency.

Specific phobia - This is the uncertainty that anxiety causes. This is caused by a specific circumstance. This fear is unreasonable. Mindfulness meditation reduces this as well.

The human brain contains a large number of neuron communicators. These communicators are linked together. These relations are intricate. "Neurotransmitters" are the communicators. There are two types of neurotransmitters. Norepinephrine is the chemical name for this. These two should be known to everyone suffering from depression. When these two factors are in harmony, we seem to feel healthy; however, when they are poor, we appear to be depressed. The majority of antidepressants target these two neurotransmitters. The problem with antidepressants is that their side effects are uncertain. Some of them are highly addictive. They do not work for everybody. Meditation has been proven to be extremely effective by scientific evidence.

Motivated students conducted research at the University of Montreal. They discovered that meditation can spontaneously boost neurotransmitters to a safe level. Serotonin and norepinephrine are the two. This will result in a neurochemical utopia. Depression cannot survive in this setting. All other depression-related problems are combated by the serotonin produced as a result of meditation. A dedicated Harvard neuroscientist performed a report on a group of meditators. He later discovered that the meditators' amygdalae shrank dramatically. The amygdalae are the parts of the brain that are in charge of depression. This component was less electrically active as well. Meditation, in a nutshell, turned off the part of the brain that is associated with depression.

As a result, meditation is the ideal treatment for those suffering from depression. We may become conscious of our negative thoughts through meditation. These negative thoughts can be a major source of anxiety. Meditation, in addition to helping us feel better, stops us from suffering depression. Depression can cause changes in the size and strength of our brains. The research was carried out on several depressed people. The researchers discovered that the test subjects' hippocampus was severely underdeveloped. The hippocampus is the portion of the brain that is responsible for memory loss and disorientation. They also discovered that the more an individual suffered from depression, the smaller the hippocampus became. They then devised a method to mitigate this effect, which led to the development of meditation. Several studies have shown that meditation practitioners have a highly developed and stable hippocampus — the more years spent meditating, the greater the hippocampal grey matter density. Simply put, the more you meditate, the bigger and stiffer your hippocampus grows. As a result, the brain rises above all levels of depression.

However, you do not have to practice meditation for many years to see results. Meditation continues to work after a few days or weeks of practice. Meditation has been used for decades to help people develop calmer, more concentrated, and healthier minds. This has been scientifically shown. Our brains shoot neurons all the time. This generates electrical signals. These signals, when combined, form "brainwave patterns." From our bodies to our emotions, introspection, and depression, we are all directly measured by brainwave patterns. The Biofeedback

Institute conducted studies on suicidal alcoholics almost thirty years ago. This study made use of alpha and theta brainwave patterns. The aim was to use these behaviors to help people recover from depression. It was discovered that their depression had reduced by 80% as a result of the therapy. Most neuroscientists are fascinated by our brains for a variety of reasons. Meditation, for example, effectively enhances alpha and theta brainwaves. For example, the EquiSync can be used to easily acquire these brainwave patterns.

Meditation has long been thought to be the key to having advanced, organized, and safe minds. A substantial amount of data has been gathered about the calming effect of meditation on depression. This evidence supports a quick and effective treatment for depression. As humans, we strive to exert control over our emotions. The "prefrontal cortex" is the portion of the brain responsible for this. Pascual-Leone discovered that this portion of the brain was underdeveloped in depressed patients after conducting studies on them. These patients struggled to keep their feelings in check. Harvard neuroscientist, Sara Lazar, demonstrated that meditation practitioners' minds had formed "prefrontal cortex gray matter."

Simply put, the more time you spend meditating, the stronger and more resilient your prefrontal cortex becomes. This results in increased emotional intelligence. This empowers you to properly balance and maintain your emotional life. According to studies, meditators are the brightest, healthiest, and happiest people on the planet.

Meditation helps to reduce sleeplessness and insomnia - One of the best sleepers in this world is the people who meditate. If there would be a race to sleep, the meditators will win without a hustle. Here we will be looking at how to use meditation to cure sleeplessness. Sleep is essential as the food we eat. Rest is almost similar to the case of food and the stomach. The human being not only requires sleep, but to sleep efficiently.

We depend on sleep for our well-being. As human beings, we all have chores. For example, people have to make a living. These activities make us exhausted, and we fatigue. Most of us tend not to get enough sleep. Scientists have been studying our sleeping brains for years. Until recently, they have now understood how it functions. The human brain is one of the big industries in the body. It produces several neurochemicals. One of the influential neurochemicals produced by the brain is melatonin. This is also referred to as the sleep hormone. It is mostly produced just before bedtime. It ensures our body gets a deep and restful sleep. This hormone has its inhibitors. Inhibitors prevent the secretion of this hormone. Stress is one of the inhibitors of melatonin. This inhibits our natural sleep cycle. For us, humans, we are fortunate to have a natural remedy.

Researchers at Rutgers University uncovered that meditators had a higher level of melatonin.

Most of the biological markers for sleep are naturally balanced through meditation. This ensures that you get a good night's sleep. The advantages are that the sleep is super deep, and you feel recharged in the morning. This gives no room for insomnia. When we are depressed, our brains tend to have beta brainwaves. The same thing also happens when we are anxious. Beta brainwaves in excess have a detrimental effect. Once they are in excess, they can prevent us from sleeping efficiently. This failure to sleep can lead to more production of beta brainwaves. This is a major complaint from many insomnia patients. This cycle repeats itself to ensure we do not fall asleep. Research shows that meditation practitioners who achieve deep state meditation tend to have a lower attack of insomnia. They also produce fewer beta brainwaves. Instead, they provide more beneficial alpha and theta brainwave patterns. Anyone wanting a good night's sleep should use meditation as his or her remedy.

Most of us tend not to sleep sometimes at night due to the never-ending list of things to do. This is a natural phenomenon. However, to some extent, it will leave us deprived of sleep, which is not an excellent factor in our lives. It can lower our energy and affect our health in return. Mindfulness meditation teaches us to be aware of the present moment. This awareness also includes our thoughts. This awareness of our body and feelings and how they affect us in the present is the primary way to calm your mind and get sleep. We can use meditation to train our bodies to be ready to sleep.

Meditation Assists in Conquering Addictions

Every member of the human race has an addiction, whether it is safe or not. Meditation is one of the most effective strategies for overcoming addiction. The function of various brain parts in addiction was discovered in a study published in the American Journal of Psychiatry. They also discovered that while people are intoxicated, the prefrontal cortex, or pleasure core, becomes involved (gets a hit). When there is a withdrawal, the same region becomes inactive. Meditation is an effective way to automatically stimulate the prefrontal cortex. Sara Lazar performed research on meditators. She discovered that meditators' neural density and prefrontal cortex were extremely involved. So, how does this relate to addiction? We may achieve natural highness through meditation. This can be accomplished by teaching the body and mind to be content. This high does not necessitate the use of caffeine or any other medications. This good feeling is not devoid of any addictive drug. According to a study conducted on patients with opioid addiction by the American journal of drug and alcohol abuse, we can maintain our addiction-free status through meditation.

Electroencephalogram Biofeedback training was provided to the patients, which includes the use of brainwave patterns. This therapy raises the patient's brainwave patterns to a higher degree of consciousness. After a year, almost 80% of the addicts were drug-free. The research also discovered that alpha and beta brainwaves predominate during meditation. This suggests that meditation can be useful in the treatment of addiction. It's entirely normal. People who are addicted have a strong desire to fulfill their cravings. It's almost too much to bear. This type of action has the potential to be self-destructive. We can resolve such behavior through meditation. Meditation keeps us from being swayed by certain stuff. This approach directs the mind's attention away from addictive thoughts. During meditation, our consciousness watches, without judging, the passing of cravings and desires. The urges begin to fade when you gain control of your mind through meditation. You are no longer under the sway of your desires.

Many addicts have been studied in terms of human behavior. Dopamine is a brain chemical discovered by scientists. When an addict takes a dose, this brain chemical is released into the bloodstream. This chemical is produced in particular areas of the brain, such as the "nucleus accumbens." When an addict crushes, dopamine levels are found to be low. This forces him or her to seek more dopamine, resulting in a vicious loop. The scientists were searching for a natural way to counteract the dopamine release activity. According to John Kennedy's research, addicts' dopamine levels increased by 60% as they meditated. Their dopamine levels were optimal and balanced. As a result, the addicts avoided crushing.

For ninety days, the University of Washington conducted studies on inmates. The inmates were addicted to drugs and alcohol. Meditation classes were provided to these inmates. They did well when it came to learning meditation. They were found to consume less of the addictive drug after ninety days. Those who kept meditating remained drug-free. Meditation is six times more effective than any other form of addiction treatment. This is an excellent example of meditation's healing ability. Sadness is the leading cause of addiction. One can never be unhappy if one lives a completely conscious life. The continuous practice of meditation leads to this state of complete consciousness.

Meditation Maintains Your Focus and Boosts Motivation

Focus and motivation are essential for one's success. In history, people have endured challenges. These challenges never made them give up. A perfect example is Dr. Seuss and his book "Green Egg and Ham." His writing was declined to publish. His book was not only rejected by one publisher, but 27 different publishers.

Another example is Oprah Winfrey. Her producer thought she was not fit for TV. With this in his mind, he ended up firing her on the spot. All these struggles did not deter these people from pursuing their dreams. This applies to any area in life. Be it an athlete, player, or politician, focus and motivation affect success considerably. The question remains how can we be motivated every time? For any successful career, there are many struggles. Some call this force that offers these struggles "resistance." This resistance maintains the status quo. Everyone in life has to fight this "resistance." To be successful, we have to beat down the giant resistance. It is everywhere, provided we are alive. To get over this giant, we can utilize the power of meditation.

There is a region in the brain called the "thalamus." This separates consciousness from the external environment. This is the main entrance to the human consciousness. This separates the stimuli that do not need high thinking to the one that requires it. High thinking regions in the brain are the cerebral cortex and subcortical areas. Our modern world has beaten our thalamus. The thalamus no longer functions properly. We are more likely to have disorders like anxiety. With this, most of the time, our brains are overloaded. By utilizing the power of meditation, we can reduce the workload on our brains. Meditation helps our gate to human consciousness; it can now rest and rejuvenate with our mind and thalamus fully functional. This allows us to think more deeply. Since we can now think deeply, we can make well thought decisions and solve our issues more efficiently. Since a highly efficient brain is a focused brain, we become more focused on our daily life activities.

By meditation, we train our brains to be focused in any situation. This allows us to recover fast from failures, making everything achievable. We can use meditation to achieve our goals. The part of the brain that keeps us motivated towards our goals is known as the "dorsolateral prefrontal cortex." A study by Italian neuroscientists in 2015 found that meditation stiffens the wiliness to work towards a goal. It also builds the ability of a person to control himself/herself. This can and will, in turn, boost our motivation. The universe always expects us to produce great things. When we focus on our objectives, that is the ignition, and we require to start doing great things.

How Can Meditation Help With Relationship Anxiety

You know you are anxious when you feel restless or tensed. Your heart may beat at an accelerated rate, and your breathing may quicken. Some people tend to feel tired and weak easily when they are anxious.

It is very important to note and respect the contributions your thoughts make to your anxiety level. Thoughts are the images, memories, beliefs, judgments, and reflections that float through your mind and give rise to anxiety. You can ask yourself: "What are the thoughts and images in my mind that keep me feeling as anxious as I feel?"

It is also important to note that fear and anxiety will never solve your problems; instead, they will worsen them. You may unknowingly be substituting practical actions for unnecessary emotions. Meditation breaks down those defenses and excuses. It will help you identify your problems and resources and help you face your relationship problems head-on.

Meditation is a practice with very many benefits. It is a way of training the mind and thought process, which will, in turn, eliminate anxiety. Ellie Shoji, a meditation expert, said that the same way physical exercise trains the body, meditation trains the mind.

This practice has more benefits than just helping us have positive thoughts and thinking; it also rejuvenates our physical and mental health. And often, when we help ourselves, we help those around us. In this way, solo meditation can positively affect a relationship.

Anxiety can be brought about by a lot of factors.

You would agree that relationships can be a very mind-boggling adventure. It is also scary sometimes. Relationships demand full exposure of your true, undiluted personalities; this will make you vulnerable to heartbreaks and abuse. So, it is normal for one to feel confused and overwhelmed. People generally feel overwhelmed when there are major and scary decisions to be made. For example, it can be scary to decide to share a dark secret with a new partner. This confusion usually causes anxiety. You can reduce any anxiety your relationship gives you through meditation. Meditation clears your mind and calms it down so you can make major decisions on your relationship effectively.

It is understandable if you feel wary about using meditation to cure your anxiety. You may find it hard to believe that a seated, quiet, and isolated activity can help strengthen your social skills, reduce your anxiety level and relationship skills, but research shows it does.

Therefore, let us show you a few ways meditation can prevent anxiety in your relationship.

Strained Communication

Communication is essential for a healthy relationship. If the communication in your relationship is strong, it can be healthy and lasting. Strained communication in relationships usually begets anxiety. Meditation can help clear this away. Imagine you are walking in a foggy place. It is difficult to see where you are going, but you simply have to keep moving forward. It will become more difficult to see through if you panic, but you will definitely see better if you are calm. This works in communication too. So much happens in a day, and one is usually tired, with a clogged mind. The more you meditate, the calmer you become, and the easier it will be to wade through the communication fog and express yourself better.

Meditation will free you from within and any hindrance to your effective communication in a relationship, which will be easy to deal with.

Toxic Personality

No sane human will want to be found in a relationship with a toxic human. Sometimes, though, the toxicity usually arises as a result of clashes in opposite personalities. You might worry that your personality is causing undue stress on your partner. This worry can cause you a lot of anxiety. You can change your existing scenario with meditation. As a human being, you must have carried your emotional and mental baggage for many years without relief. Apart from a series of outbursts caused by emotional imbalances, this might even cost you your health. Just like snakes that shed their skin and dogs that shake off water from their fur, you need to shake off the baggage you have carried around before you can successfully rejuvenate yourself. When your mind is free of constant worry, you would find it easy to be happy and, in turn, spread that happiness to others. What you have inside you is what you would reflect on others around you. This will ease your anxiety, and you will find yourself becoming your partners' peace. Your partner will also feel compelled to reciprocate, and you would move on in life, a happier and motivated person.

Former Relationship

This is usually a great cause of strained relationships and needless anxiety. Meditation helps you heal from any past heartbreak you might have experienced. During meditation, the mind is content and alert so it can greatly heal the body, heart, and soul. It harmonizes the mind and triggers the healing process.

Gratefulness

A very strong incentive to meditate for a good relationship is its impact on your perspective. Meditation helps you control and regulate your emotions, and this power will help you keep a positive perspective. You will find it easier to stay grateful. Gratitude is a very strong indicator of a long-lasting and healthy relationship. Research proves that, over some time, you will get used to the things you own and the people that are constantly around you, and you will tend to take those things and those people for granted. As a result, you may get to the point where you may focus your energy on your partner's negative attributes and even forget why you fell in love with them in the first place.

Grateful people are usually more satisfied in their relationships and feel closer to one another. Staying grateful will help you stay focused and appreciative of your partner's good qualities. Your partner, in turn, will feel appreciated, and the bond you share will be strengthened.

Work-related Stress

You might be going through and experiencing a lot of stress at work. Unfortunately, though, you might bring your stress home to your partner. Inevitably, your partner will get the short end of the stick: a bad temperament, difficult mood swings, and a lack of affection, etc. After a while, this continued pattern will lead to a tense atmosphere in the home and widen the gulf between partners. A research was conducted with veterans returning from war. They were chosen because of the large amount of stress these veterans are known to be under. They used a simple breathing-based meditation known as 'sugarcane Kaiya' yoga, and their stress and anxiety level dropped drastically. Suppose you can take bold steps in dealing with your stress by using this kind of simple practice. In that case, you not only will curb your own stress, but also help preserve your relationships with your partners.

It Keeps You Positive

Meditation helps you stay positive and charismatic. It makes you more present, more focused, more productive, and even more creative. Your ability to learn and reason outside the box will improve. Positive emotions indeed help you connect freely with others. It helps us be more open, more approachable, and even solidifies our feelings of connection with other people, even strangers. To explain better, you will realize that you are less likely to start up a conversation with the person behind you at a bank on the days you feel anxious and stressed. This is because stress makes us selfish and more self-focused. However, though, on the days you feel great, happy, and excited, you are more likely to start a conversation or share a joke with a stranger or even notice if someone needs help going through a door. Research shows that laughter, which only occurs when you feel positive, makes you more receptive to new persons and helps you create and strengthen relationships. Also, it helps you endure in the face of difficulty. Difficulty can come in the form of a challenging relationship. All of us will face problems in our relationships, but only some of us have natural resilience and the ability to endure and bounce back quickly. Thousands of researches will show that meditation is a strong way to improve happiness and your general well-being. By helping with anxiety and even depression, it can help keep you in a positive frame of mind that has enormous benefits.

Your Connection

As noted earlier, after a while, partners tend to feel disconnected from each other. In research conducted on loving-kindness and compassion based on meditation, it was realized that these types of meditation can greatly help partners feel more empathetic and connected. Meditation can help train and help you to feel more compassionate and loving. Other research shows that empathy and compassion contribute a lot, positively, to your health, well-being, and happiness: improved happiness, decreased anxiety and depression, and even longer life, not to mention stronger and healthier relationships with other persons. To further convince you of the effectiveness of meditation, let us consider "Research Works Carried out on Meditation and Generalized Anxiety Disorder (GAD)."

This research aimed to prove the benefits of meditation on generalized anxiety disorder and the positive results. In 2013, a random yet regulated test was carried out with 93 people diagnosed with GAD. These people had to go through 8 weeks of manualized mindfulness-based stress reduction in a group program and an attention control or stress management education test.

After the test, it was obvious that mindfulness-based stress reduction (MBSR) had significantly larger anxiety reduction for three out of the four study forms. These people also showed a more profound increase in positive self-motivating statements.

Difficulties in This Meditation

There are several detractors to meditation. You might find that it is hard to meditate or be mindful. You might find it difficult to concentrate without letting the critique voice speak, or you may feel too busy or restless as though there is simply too much to do to be lounging around, breathing in and out. People are wired differently. Some people simply find it difficult to just do nothing. They are constantly on the move, and they are used to it. Sometimes, you might realize that you cannot prevent difficult thoughts from taking over even when you try to relax.

The best advice that will help to overcome these obstacles comes in two ways:

Respect the Process

You should understand and recognize that this will take some time. You will not become an expert at this in a day. When you first start meditating, you will feel strange. Your mind will bug you, make you feel that you are wasting your time, just sitting around there doing nothing literally. You will even get angry and fed up. Even with all this, though, religiously continue with it. It will definitely get better. Do not expect your very first meditation practice to be easy at all; it may not. Funny as it sounds, it does take practice to master the art of doing absolutely nothing. In the end, it will become easier. Create time

Since you have identified that meditation will take time, it is best to make time. Put in a time for it on your schedule just like you put in a job or an appointment. Do not make it an option not to practice. There is no reason why the practice should be skipped for a day. Just discipline yourself. Tell yourself that you need to get it done. Most times, when you find that you have got a lot of things to do and achieve and you still try to fit in time for a calm moment, you will discover, later, that that calm moment helped you to go back to your day more aware and faster at solving problems.

Update a diary with records on your growth and truthfully indicate if your anxiety is reducing. After a short while of constant meditation, you should ask yourself questions like: When anxious thoughts flashed through your mind, were you able to examine them without criticizing or judging them? Did you succeed in acquiring a moment of focused observation? Did you feel calm, relaxed, and aware? If you are still plagued with troubling thoughts and anxiety that are repetitive and harsh after a while, go ahead and talk with your doctor about other treatment options.

How to Practice Meditation for Generalized Anxiety Disorder (GAD)

If you are suffering from generalized anxiety disorder, performing constant daily meditation can help you overcome anxiety and reduce increased tension in your body. Yoga has a lot to do with meditation. If you have ever taken a yoga class, you have taken a good first step and are already on the right path to achieving the peace you seek.

Again, at first, you will not need a whole lot of time to meditate. A few minutes will be maybe all you need. Make efforts to make out a few minutes each day to meditate. As you become more and more familiar with the process and figure out how to relax and discover what it feels like to be calm, you can slowly increase that time.

GAD is simply unrelenting worry, worry that will not go away. Meditation helps you learn to live with those worries and thoughts without giving them the power to upset you. When you finally achieve that, your distress is more likely to reduce.

What Exactly is Meditation?

Meditation is a straightforward method of unwinding the mind. It is one of the simplest ways to temporarily remove yourself from your mind's inner chaos and gain a rational understanding of what is going on inside it. It is the most effective method for untangling complicated thoughts.

However, it is, above all, a means of bringing harmony and tranquility into your life.

We all have problems in this race called life. Within our brains, a hundred different things are going on. According to most conservative figures, the human mind has about 50,000 thoughts a day. Even if only a small percentage of these thoughts are negative, upsetting, or problematic, they can wreak havoc on one's life. Unfortunately, most of us fall into the category of having more than a small percentage of such negative feelings. As a result of these reflections, the mind is continually devising strategies and counterstrategies. It is not something you can actively regulate. You can find it difficult to shush your mind, even for a short period. Such thoughts will keep you awake at night. The more you try to drive these feelings away, the more violent they get.

Meditation is a technique for temporarily quieting the mind. It's an easy exercise that will help you gain control of your mind and emotions. You would be able to literally clear your mind for some time before refilling it with optimistic thoughts. The time you spend in meditation allows you to choose the ideas you want to focus on critically. You can isolate each negative thought in your mind and choose to discard it forever. Meditation will give you tremendous influence over your thinking process and, as a result, over your life.

It can be a successful treatment for the sorrows, worries, anxieties, feelings of hate, and general confusion that you are experiencing in your life. It is one of the most effective methods for fully transforming the mind. You would be able to attain thoughtless consciousness. This will not only clear your mind, but will also make you relaxed and inwardly centered.

Meditation is a technique for determining the source of mental disorders. It is a deep state of mind in which you can see things critically and make better decisions. The best part about meditation is that you don't need something special to do it. All you have to do is sit, stand, or walk quietly. Once you're comfortable with the procedure, you can do it anytime. You will have incredible influence over your life and will be able to experience the bliss you have been seeking. You'll feel happier, more fulfilled, and more at ease.

Modern life has devolved into a race in which we are all competing without a clear objective in mind. There is no winner in this race since there is no finish line. Meditation will provide you with the necessary understanding to enjoy the race.

How Does Meditation Work?

To a bystander, a person in the meditative state may look like an idle person sitting in a cross-legged posture with eyes closed. There is no complexity. One doesn't even need to be in this position to meditate. You can meditate while sitting on a chair, while walking, or even while lying on the ground.

The body may look inactive while in the meditative state, but the mind is very active. You can unfold some of the most complex mysteries of the mind in the meditative state.

On the physical level, meditation strongly influences the activity of the brain. It helps in clearing the mind and also brings objective focus. Every important thought that comes to your brain leads to a certain type of chemical reaction. The positive thoughts have a calming effect. Happy thoughts lead to the secretion of chemicals that suppress anger and anxiety. When you have many negative, stressful, and fearful thoughts, stress hormones increase in your body. This will not only cause emotional trouble, but will also weaken your immune system.

A person trying to lose weight will find it really difficult to burn fat while in a stressful, emotional state. The reason being the increased production of the stress hormone. This hormone keeps the body in a constant fat storage mode. Meditation is a wonderful way to relax your mind as well as the nervous system. It increases activity in the specific regions in the brain, associated with decreasing anxiety and depression. Your body also develops a better tolerance for pain. Memory, self-awareness, and the ability for goal-setting also improves with the help of meditation.

Our brain, in its active state, produces beta waves that are fast and choppy. The thoughts in this state can be jumbled up. There are too many thoughts at the same time with very little control over them. However, while in the meditative state, the brain starts producing slow alpha waves. These waves cause relaxation. The stress level starts to go down. The rambling of thought also goes down. You will start feeling greater control over your mind in this state. These waves are associated with feelings of love, positivity, and happiness. The level of alpha waves keeps increasing as one starts to practice meditation for longer.

Meditation can bring physical change in the shape and size of your brain. Studies conducted on long-time practitioners have demonstrated that meditation leads to increased gray matter in certain brain areas.

Two important areas are:

Insular Cortex: This area is associated with an awareness of breathing and heartbeat. The longer you meditate, the better will be your breathing and heart. This would mean that your body would be in a better position to carry oxygen and carbon dioxide. You would have better immunity against diseases.

Premotor Cortex: This area regulates attention, emotions, and thoughts. Your learning power and memory will also improve if the gray matter in this area gets denser. You would have better control over your emotions and thoughts.

The amygdala in your brain deals with stress, fear, and anxiety. Studies have clearly demonstrated that meditation can help in decreasing the gray matter in this area. It can greatly help in reducing stress, fear, high blood pressure, and immunity-related disorders.

With practice, your brain can also start producing gamma waves. These waves can help in bringing deep concentration and an unwavering focus. Apart from the physiological stuff, meditation also helps you develop a better ability to deal with your thoughts and emotions.

Our mind remains mostly confused between wants and needs. The problems begin when it starts treating both interchangeably. Our expectations from people, jobs, relationships, personal wealth, and other such things are always high, and when they aren't met, we start having negative thoughts. Meditation helps you in viewing your thoughts objectively. You will be able to understand the true value of things and also judge the futility of wants. This can make life much simpler. Most essential things are not even required in life, but we waste our lives pursuing them. We simply follow them endlessly because we see others around us doing the same. We acquire the herd mentality and get involved in the mind-numbing rat race. Meditation helps you objectively analyze your thoughts, needs, and wants to choose the best course of action. You'd find yourself much more calm, relaxed, and peaceful after meditation sessions. Decision-making would become easier, and your mind wouldn't constantly be battling decision fatigue. Your perspective about things would improve, along with your ability to look at things objectively.

Why Should You Practice Meditation?

Most of the things that you might have tried to date take some time to show results. Meditation is a unique practice that starts showing results instantaneously. The day you begin meditation, you will start experiencing a positive change in your stress and anxiety levels. You will feel more relaxed and calm. There is a feeling of joy that emerges from inside when you start practicing meditation. Besides these, meditation has many more benefits that you will experience as you start practicing it for longer.

Makes you Happier: Meditation has a great calming effect on the mind. You start feeling relaxed and joyful. There is a feeling of inner bliss. The flow of constructive thoughts increases in the brain; hence, meditators feel really joyful and happy.

Reduces Anxiety, Stress, and Depression: Our brain has a specific amygdala regulating stress, anxiety, and depression. Studies have shown that meditation can lead to a reduction in the size of these areas. If you practice meditation regularly, you will notice a significant reduction in your stress and anxiety levels.

Instant Results: The positive impact of meditation can be noticed from the very first session. You will start feeling relaxed and calm from the very beginning. You wouldn't have to wait for months to notice the positive effect.

Improves Sleep: Meditation has a very strong impact on your sleep patterns. The people who meditate find significant improvement in their sleep. They can sleep better and wake up more relaxed and calm. Sleep deprivation is a problem that affects many people these days. It not only increases stress levels, but also has a severe impact on overall health. Meditation can help a lot in this area. It helps you fall asleep much faster.

Sharpens Memory: Meditation improves memory. Your mind gets trained to live in the present and analyze thoughts objectively. This also means that it learns the ways to retain important things strongly. Your memory sharpens over a while as you meditate.

Brings Clarity: One of the most significant advantages of meditation is that it helps you achieve a state of thoughtless awareness. This is the state in which you can look at all the things in your mind in a non-judgmental way. Your perspective improves, and you can get better clarity of thoughts. The reactionary thought process stops, and you can look at things objectively.

The Impacts of Meditation on Your Daily Life

As individuals, the first thing that we all crave in life is — peace.

But, peace is a broad term and one that leads to an endless list of questions.

How do we define peace?

What gives us peace?

And most importantly, why do we crave it?

All of these questions are pertinent, and all of them have weight. You will begin to realize it is even more as you embark on your personal journey into the human mind searching for it. However, as you seek peace, it is important that you first understand how the human mind works and, more importantly, how meditation has multiple positive effects on the human mind, body, and soul.

Building Self-Awareness

For starters, let's focus on self-awareness.

Take a minute and honestly ask yourself how aware you are of how your body reacts to specific situations. How do you react to light? How do you react to fear? How do you react to happy events? Take a minute and identify each of these physical manifestations of your mind and evaluate why do you react in this way? Have you always acted in a specific manner? What has changed, if anything?

You may notice that as you go through these questions in your mind, other questions and thoughts will enter your mind that you didn't anticipate. This is actually very typical and natural. At times, if you think that a specific thought or specific trigger will cause your mind to think or work in a specific manner, in reality, it doesn't necessarily process the information in any specific way. This is why reverse psychology works on certain individuals and backfires on others as not all people react to the same form of stimulus in the same manner. Meditation allows you to practice introspection and truly identify how your mind reacts to specific triggers. It's almost as if your mind is doing a mental inventory of how you think, how you process, and most importantly, how you react.

Try to think of meditation as a form of mental yoga — here, the objective is to forge a stronger link between the mind and body. This ensures that your mind is more aware of how your body is responding specifically to cues. Meditation helps us understand our own individual sense of awareness. Helping ground us in the present moment allows us to act and think in a way that keeps us in the present.

Reducing Stress and Anxiety

This is just one benefit —meditation is not intended to simply enhance one's sense of self. A major reason why so many people get involved in meditation is that they wish to use the practice to cure unwanted stress and anxiety that they might be dealing with. Let's simplify this, shall we?

Why do you think you are invested in meditation?

What do you feel unsure or nervous about starting your meditation program?

Try answering this instead — in the past week, what are five negative things that have impacted the way you act, think, and react? Make a shortlist in a separate journal. Have you listed them for yourself? Good! Now, ask yourself how often one of these thoughts has controlled your mind. Let's say you feel unhappy at work — how often have you thought of quitting? A lot?

How often do you think about how badly you want to change jobs? Almost always?

Most importantly, how often have you done something that would help you change your job, or extract yourself from that toxic work environment? Odds are you just said never very quietly under your breath. Whether or not you feel like you are ready to admit your thoughts to other people, you know exactly how often you sometimes obsess over the negatives in your life. Do you ever wonder why you don't feel comfortable telling other people how often these negative thoughts come to your mind?

Think about it - if you don't like admitting how you are thinking, odds are that you already know, subconsciously or at some level, that what you are doing isn't good for you. Remember that while negative things will continue to happen in your life, how far you allow that negativity to spread into your personal space is a decision that you are constantly making. There is always a more productive way to deal with negative thoughts — if you feel you are stuck in a bad job, instead of obsessing over the job's negative features, train your mind to focus on the way out. Line up new job interviews, consider talking to the human resources department or a supervisor; the point here is to actively do something instead of just letting things happen to you.

Taking control of your negativity is a key part of ensuring that you lead a healthier and happier life. This negativity is what breeds stress and causes anxiety to build in your mind. So, if you really want to live a stress-free, healthier, and most importantly, happier life, you are going to want to start by finding a way to reduce your stress levels and train your mind to focus on productive activities instead of the anxiety triggers that you have built for yourself.

Honing Mental Clarity

Another common issue many individuals tend to have to deal with is — the lack of clarity predominant in today's world. For the most part, research has shown that multiple mental disciplines, such as yoga and meditation, can help control the mind and improve it. Conditions such as ADHD, which is a form of attention deficiency, have shown significant improvement with meditation and meditation-based activities.

While it is common knowledge that physical exercise can help keep the body in shape, people tend to forget that the brain needs the exact same thing. Neuro exercises or mental training activities can potentially keep our brain in shape and can also weed out certain undesirable mental characteristics, such as depressive thoughts or anxiety.

One of the fundamental issues currently being studied by scientists is the subject of neuroplasticity. What is neuroplasticity, you may ask? Well, simply put, scientists have begun to discover that, contrary to popular opinion, an individual's brain is not shaped at the time of their birth — in contrast, the brain is actually constantly growing and learning, which is why it is possible to actually change our brains to specific forms of mental training. For example, one can retrain the brain to alter or improve multiple personality quirks, such as how attentive you are, how happy you are, how angry you are, etc.

Instead of considering emotions such as happiness, anger, or disappointment, individual reactions think of them as skills. You can train your mind so that you are more skilled at being happy or positive, although odds are you have subconsciously been training your mind to be the exact opposite. Neuroscientist Richard Davison of the University of Wisconsin conducted a three-month research program on the impacts of the Vipassana form of Buddhist meditation that deals with increased mental clarity and improving sensory awareness. On completion, he found that volunteers who had received Vipassana meditation as a form of mental training were much faster in their ability to identify and focus on detailed information. In contrast, individuals who had not participated in the training seemed less clear and less stable in their ability to retain information. Thus, meditation is now being seen as a form of mental exercise that helps individuals take advantage of the human brain's plasticity in a quantifiable and scientific manner.

Building Focus and Fortitude

However, it is not just mental clarity that is affected by meditation. In fact, a large part of meditation deals with building focus. While the science of the issue has clearly established that meditation can help enhance mental clarity by playing with the mind's neural plasticity, it also does so on a more chemical level by releasing specific hormones to counter your stress levels.

When you are stressed out, your body releases certain hormones to let your mind know that it is overloaded. Once your mind starts to register that you are stressed out, the body releases adrenaline because it thinks that your body now needs more energy to help get you through these backlogged tasks. The only problem here is that adrenaline can work against you. Theoretically, adrenaline should help you get better and do your tasks quicker and better. Adrenaline serves as an important function in our bodies, but unless we learn to control stress, adrenaline works against us. Instead of helping us get through stressful moments, excessive adrenaline instead increases anxiety and multiplies our stress reaction.

Keep in mind the release of adrenaline in your body is a physical reaction to fear or danger, or some sort of immediate desperate need — this is a physical reaction that has been passed on to us from our ancestors, who, at the time, needed that extra bit of energy to fend off predators or to stay alive. Imagine having that level of pressure on you every day because you cannot distinguish between a life-and-death situation and a workplace crisis. Your body simply doesn't know the difference.

This, of course, is where meditation steps in. Meditation gives us a sense of self-worth and power so that when we are faced with a challenge, we are not immediately dropping the ball and going into "danger" mode — instead, we are calmly teaching ourselves to cope, which, in turn, allows our brain to focus and develop better-coping strategies.

Have you ever given yourself a social media detox? Is your immediate reaction after you wake up to check Facebook? One of the first things you might want to do is slowly detach from your phone or social media distractions over the next seven days.

Meditation teaches your brain to do the same thing in terms of the topics you are focusing on. By slowly teaching yourself to focus on the factors you would like, such as positive outcomes, you simultaneously build your mental fortitude. You're training your brain to not go into panic mode at the slightest thing. At the same time, you are also teaching yourself how to react to those smaller yet persistent mental problems you face daily. Win-win!

Emotional Intelligence

So, what else does meditation help with? Well, for starters, it is also an extremely important tool in the development of emotional intelligence. As you begin to become more aware of yourself and react to specific situations, you will also realize that you are attuned to how people react to those same situations. This form of awareness is also commonly known as emotional intelligence and is currently considered extremely high value. Indeed, some scientists have begun to prefer emotional intelligence evaluation over evaluating one intelligence quotient to determine a person's potential.

While you probably ask yourselves multiple times whether or not you are good enough or smart enough, odds are you probably don't ask yourself if you are compassionate enough or if you are a good listener. If you are familiar with the television program, The Big Bang Theory, you've probably seen that the protagonist Sheldon Cooper has been portrayed as an individual with an extremely high IQ but extraordinarily low EQ factor. In later seasons, this impacts his career growth, as well as his personal life. This is actually extremely common - no matter how smart you are, you will find that you will require a certain amount of emotional intelligence to truly succeed in life.

Start asking yourself the following questions to gauge what your emotional intelligence levels are:

Are you generally a calm person? Are you capable of maintaining this calm in stressful situations?

Would you consider yourself to be compassionate? Are you well attuned to the needs of others?

In your opinion, do you have a tendency to make good decisions?

Are you capable of listening to what other people have to say? Do you take people's opinions into consideration? Do you believe that you have a positive influence on the people around you?

Are you an impulsive person? How impulsive do you consider yourself to be, on a scale of 1 to 10?

What is your standard mindset — happy or sad?

Were the answers that you just provided generally negative in nature? If so, odds are you have a low EQ; the good news is it doesn't really matter how low your EQ is because you can actually build on your EQ levels through meditation. The act of meditation helps you detach from negative thoughts, but it is also known to help you assess and attune yourself to other people's emotions. Poker players, for instance, are known to have extremely high emotional intelligence levels; their advanced emotional intelligence allows them to 'read' emotions, such as fear or hesitation in their opponents, which, in turn, enables them to make better plays.

Most importantly, your emotional intelligence levels will help you deal with years of emotional baggage that have burdened your inner mind control. Gone are the days that you couldn't control your temper. With the help of meditation, you can now actively deal with your anxiety, your depression, and your negative thought patterns, replacing them with solid reasoning skills and problem-solving capabilities.

Relaxing the Mind

And finally, one of the least appreciated and yet possibly one of the most beneficial attributes of meditation — mental relaxation. Think about it...when was the last time you gave your brain a break? Keep in mind that going away on holiday does not count. When was the last time that you sat still for 15 minutes and did absolutely nothing? You didn't mentally list the tasks you have to do; you didn't make decisions about what you're going to need for dinner. You didn't worry about ten different things that happened today — you literally did nothing.

Let's be honest; odds are it's been a while. Lucky for you, meditation is actually known to trigger the relaxation response in mind. Any time you spend meditating is time you are spending allowing your brain to go into a state of absolute relaxation.

Why is this important? The more relaxed your brain is, the easier it is for you to fall asleep, manage your stress levels, and reduce your anxiety. Think of it as your emotional balance; by relaxing your brain, you train it to maintain better emotional equilibrium, allowing you to become a more balanced individual.

Chapter 14: Getting Rid of Your Negative Thoughts

Buddhism is the kind of religion that always encourages a complete and utter focus on the positive aspects of life, which are meant to encourage and inspire you to attain a more peaceful mindset. Therefore, this chapter will focus on how you can clear up your bundled collection of negative thoughts and convert them into positive energy.

But before explaining the strategies, you must first understand what "Negative Self-Talk" really is.

What is Self-Talk?

To put it most simply, self-talk is what we say to ourselves. People sometimes vocalize their self-talk out loud, but by far, the majority of self-talk that happens in people takes place inside their heads, privately. When I talk about "self-talk" throughout this book, I always mean both kinds - word thoughts and vocalizations. They have equal importance since they both reveal a lot about what we think of ourselves and what we think of the world we live in.

This personal inner monologue can be positive or negative, and it always combines conscious thoughts with unconscious beliefs about ourselves and the events and circumstances of the world we find ourselves in.

As we shall see in more detail in later sections of this book, positive self-talk can be really beneficial in several important ways like supporting the health of the body, keeping motivated, reducing depression, helping us to achieve life goals, calming our fears, and boosting our motivation and confidence.

Negative Self-Talk (NST) also has effects on our well-being too - negative effects. We'll get into these more deeply in later sections too. Inappropriate self-critical self-talk is, unfortunately, a part of human nature. Such negative talk can often convince people not to try (and hence fail right out of the gate). Saying things like, "I can't," or "I'm a failure," or "I don't deserve XYZ," are classic examples of a self-defeating critical inner voice, and we will learn how to undo these kinds of negative self-talk habits later on.

There is a difference between self-reflection and negative self-talk. Some people find their negative self-talk motivating in that it galvanizes them and motivates them to do better. But, the truth is that negative self-talk is not constructive by definition. In the long run, it will harm people's confidence.

On the other hand, self-reflection is a much more constructive activity because it is the act of looking honestly and consciously at one's behavior and beliefs and questioning those beliefs to improve one's being and station in life. This is completely different from negative critical self-banter, which is almost always completely unconscious and does not identify weak points as sources of opportunity for positive change and growth. Critical negative self-talk might motivate some people in the short-term. Still, it can never lead to sustained benefit in the long run because it never looks for solutions or positive adaptation — ultimately, negative thinking patterns serve to undermine a person's happiness. It doesn't motivate us to make positive changes and grow as people. This book will encourage you to be self-reflective, but it will never encourage you to engage in negative self-talk and thinking. For now, it is helpful to realize that the way we speak to ourselves matters because there are very real consequences to viewing ourselves overly critically, as opposed to being our own best friend.

Your inner monologue gives your brain a way to interpret and process your daily experiences — the narrative you hold with yourself will be based on your conscious thoughts in combination with your unconscious beliefs, biases, and assumptions. Suppose you listen carefully enough, and you know what to look for. In that case, you may discover that your inner monologue can be very revealing of your own nature and tendencies. Becoming conscious of your inner dialogue is the first step you will need to take to undo negative self-talk habits and then engineer a positive relationship with yourself and your self-conversation habits.

Without being aware of your own negative self-talk, you will not be able to catch yourself 'in the act' of being self-defeating. Suppose you notice it and know what type of NST habits you are guilty of doing. In that case, you can learn effective strategies to undo your negative habits. Before we get to practical solutions, we do need a map of the terrain.

What Exactly is Negative Self-Talk?

"Self-talk" is the recording that plays over and over in our minds. It's the information that we tell ourselves repeatedly. It's the message that we remind ourselves of when we're trying to develop some perspective on our surroundings, circumstances, and how we fit into the contexts we find ourselves in.

Self-talk, in its root form, doesn't necessarily need to be something negative. There are many occasions when our self-talk can be rather positive in nature. When you acknowledge in your mind that "I'm having a good day," or "That person seems to like me," you're engaging in some level of positive self-talk. But, in my experience, I haven't seen too many people make an appointment to speak with a counselor because they felt like they were struggling with too much "positivity" or because they weren't sure why they felt so "happy all the time."

One of the patterns I have observed in my roles as pastor, counselor, and professor is that many of the people who come to me for counsel or advice struggle with a high degree of negative self-talk. They feel stuck, and they often feel quite discouraged by it. Their minds swirl with a flood of negative thoughts about themselves, and they typically suffer in silence for many years before doing something about it.

When a person struggles with negative self-talk, their mind engages in a regular pattern of reminding them of various negative things. Self-talk tends to be rather repetitive in nature. For starters, they will probably spend long periods dwelling on their shortcomings. They will keep pointing out where they fell short of some perceived or arbitrary standard in their mind.

From there, they'll take some time to re-live and re-hash past mistakes. They'll go over the scenarios and the conversations that took place in their lowest moments. They'll remind themselves of just how embarrassed they felt at the time and then convince themselves that this is all other people think about when they're thinking of them.

Then they'll take some time to dwell on their imperfections. This may take place each morning as they look in the mirror and make preparations for the day. They'll dwell on the size of their nose or their complexion. They'll stare at their hair and wish something was different about it. They'll dwell on their size and tell themselves that they're too fat, short, oddly shaped, etc. Mind you, all these perceived imperfections are born from arbitrary standards of beauty and years of comparison.

When they aren't feeding their mind negative comments about their imperfections, they'll take some time to focus on their limitations - all the things that they wish they could know, do, experience, have, etc., but they don't have as of yet. They convince themselves that they will only experience happiness and true satisfaction once these limitations are eradicated.

Does any of this sound familiar to you? What does all of this illustrate? In essence, the bulk of our negative self-talk comes from adopting a worldly standard and worldly values as the primary standard through which we filter our thinking. Our negative self-talk is rooted in our circumstances from a fleshly perspective instead of from our Lord's perspective. When we engage in this thinking, we start to believe that temporary matters are eternal realities. And as is the case with all beliefs, our beliefs inform and influence our behaviors.

The beliefs that become ingrained in our minds because of our negative self-talk influence how we treat ourselves. If you continually repeat falsehoods and negative statements to yourself, you'll eventually begin to live out those statements. You'll treat yourself poorly. You'll give up on your goals. You'll stop striving in the areas in which God has gifted you to serve.

Your false beliefs will also impact how you react to others. Instead of conveying an example of faith and optimism in Christ, you'll convey a negative perspective. Instead of filtering criticism through the lens of what God's word says is true of you, you'll begin to agree with those who paint you with the brush of their destructive words. Instead of being patient with the weaknesses of others, you'll treat them harshly and impatiently because you've never learned how to be patient with yourself and your own weaknesses.

It really has a way of becoming your dominant perspective instead of a temporary nuisance. Once it's allowed to take root in your mind, it starts to spread to all areas of your thinking until it begins to dominate your worldview.

What Are the Different Types of Negative Self-Talk?

According to the literature, there are four main kinds of self-talk categories and many other less commonly occurring ones. The four main ones are known as "Personalizing," "Catastrophizing,"

"Filtering," and "Polarizing" types of negative self-talk.

Each type or category of negative self-talk is usually labeled according to its characteristic, negativity, or style pattern. In addition to the four most common negative self-talk categories, there are actually many other slightly different forms of negative self-talk in many people, albeit less common than the main four categories.

In the next section, I will explore these four main types of negative self-talk, and then I'll describe all the rest of them too so that you can begin to cultivate your own inner awareness of when they arise in you.

To recognize negative self-talk, it is very helpful to know your inner psychological terrain beforehand - and having some labels and tools to help identify different kinds of negative self-talk within you is the perfect first step to recognizing your inner psychological terrain.

The Four Main Categories of Negative Self-Talk

Personalizing

"It's not you; it's me."

Taking responsibility for things in your life is usually considered a good thing, especially when you recognize that you have done some objective factual wrong. However, taking appropriate responsibility is quite different from inappropriately taking things personally based on your thinking. What is meant by "personalizing" negative self-talk here is the act of unrealistically taking responsibility for negative outcomes excessively.

What happens in people who have an excessive, inappropriate sense of personalization is that they blame themselves for being the cause of every little bad thing that happens to them or someone else. This is a poor habit to have because, in most cases, your assessment that it was solely your fault is often completely factually incorrect — just plain false. Most situations in life are complex and multifactorial. Most bad things happen to people due to factors they could have controlled in combination with many factors completely out of their control. People who have the negative habit of over-personalizing tend to ignore all the other factors that were not under their control in favor of beating up their own self-image and placing the blame squarely on their own shoulders.

A classic example includes having a big blow-out argument with a friend and then deciding that you were the one to blame and apologizing, even when the blame should be shared.

Another classic example of personalized overthinking is when a friend or partner chooses not to spend time with you by declining a date or event plan. Most healthy and well-adjusted people cultivate healthy friendships, and they know that their friends care for them. The person who does not overly personalize events or behavior doesn't take the decline personally, as if it were a judgment of their quality and value as a person. But, in people who compulsively talk to themselves negatively by overly personalizing people's behavior around them, this can feel like a hurtful rejection — the reason why they did/said XYZ is because, "I'm just not amazing enough," "it's my fault," "I'm a terrible person," and so on.

Another good example is when you text your group of friends in a group chat on social media, and your friends take much longer to reply than normally. If you start thinking, "Oh, they must be angry with me," "they don't like me," "they don't want to be friends anymore...," then you would be guilty of over-personalizing their slow response time.

99 times out of 100 the slow response time will have absolutely nothing to do with you at all, and if you didn't take tiny things so personally, you wouldn't feel so bad about yourself typically,

people are busy, enjoying their own lives and not really thinking of you at all; which is good, healthy, and normal. When they get to it, they'll respond, but their tardiness will have nothing to do with who you are as a person, especially if you really are friends.

Imagine being at a party and overhearing a conversation between your friends sitting in the next room. Imagine they are complaining about someone, sharing negative events and things about that person. Over-personalized people are almost always going to assume that they are being discussed in this situation, even when there is no good evidence pointing out that the conversation subject is you. People who have the unconscious negative habit of over-personalizing events and situations fear that things happen because of how horrible or worthless they think they are. This is the classic characteristic of over-personalizing self-talk, and it is very bad for your self-esteem because it distorts the way you interpret life situations.

Tip - First Steps to Reduce Overly Personalized Negative Self-Talk (NST)

To begin to deal with these kinds of social over-personalizing self-talk, you will need to be aware of your inner feelings and thoughts, and catch them as they arise. That is the first crucial step that must be taken to deal with any type of NST.

Once you notice that you are over-personalizing, then you can pause, after which you could ask yourself a few well-placed questions like, "Is this true?" "Do I know, for sure, that the reason why they are doing XYZ is because of something about me?" "Am I really to blame?"

This beginning strategic tip is actually a form of 'reality test' because it forces you to stop your negative thought processes and start being critical by measuring your automatic negative assumptions against what you actually know about the present situation. It is a process of 'checking in' to reality and the hard objective facts.

Even though you might still feel emotionally fearful that your negative self-thoughts are true, the process of challenging those thoughts, paying attention to reality, recognizing what you actually factually know, and then evaluating the truth of those negative thoughts can actually interrupt personalization in its tracks. This is because engaging the brain's critical thinking areas tends to move your brain activity away from the emotion and fear centers to the prefrontal cortex (the part of the brain responsible for planning and abstract reasoning). Doing some critical internal thought inquiry actually changes the way your brain functions and can lead to a massive reduction in anxiety — which helps to see the situation with clarity and objectivity; it also interrupts the stream of negative thinking too.

Some of the questions you could consider asking include:

Is there any evidence supporting the thought that I am somehow to blame, responsible, or a bad person?

Did the negative thoughts about myself come from facts right here right now, or am I interpreting events negatively without knowing the full facts?

What alternative explanations could combat my interpretation? Why assume the worst when I could assume something more positive instead and feel great about who I am and how my friends and acquaintances see me?

Reality testing and challenging your thoughts and assumptions in the moments that arise takes a bit of practice. You will need to be aware of what you're thinking and feeling in the moment to catch it and interrogate your mind consciously. Don't worry if you don't catch it the first ten times, keep reminding yourself to be vigilant, and then you will catch yourself indulging in negative over-personalization at some point. Once you catch it even once, it won't be as hard to catch it the next time — gradually, you can eliminate this nasty form of self-deprecation and enjoy friends, family, and social gatherings without much of the stress and anxiety that often comes with poor negative self-talk in these situations.

Catastrophizing

"I am doomed - the little things told me so."

Catastrophizing is when we let minor mishaps in our day completely ruin our inner emotional states. Often people assume the worst outcomes and then become angry, despondent, sad, demotivated, or depressed as a result. People with this negative habit often become defeated and pessimistic about future outcomes based on something tiny not going as expected.

Some people say that we should "expect the worst," because then, "...you won't be disappointed by people or life."

I can't tell you how many people have said this very thing to me throughout my life, and almost always, these people tend to be grumpy, unhappy, diminished, and emotionally impoverished shadows of who they could be.

A good example of catastrophizing is when you get stuck in traffic and assume it will take the maximum time for you to get to work or home. Assuming the worst about being stuck in traffic leads to assuming the worst about the rest of your day.

A person who catastrophizes tends to emphasize extreme negative future consequences based on present events — unreasonably so. They do not entertain the most likely outcomes, nor do they fantasize as much about positive outcomes as they do about negative ones — they focus only on the worst ones. It's like thinking that the world will end after you spill some coffee on your shirt while driving — it is a negative pattern of anticipation in response to something small going poorly.

Why would anyone assume the worst will happen? There are very few situations where 'assuming the worst' is actually a good practice. An example of "assuming the worst" that makes sense and adds value might be an engineering and designing public infrastructure. In that case, one has to assume the worst and put conservative safety margins to counteract potential catastrophic failure. To do this, engineers must assume that failure is inevitable and then do everything they can to reasonably limit disaster in those situations.

The above kind of prudent planning based on 'what could go wrong' is completely appropriate when planning a space rocket trip, safety margins for elevators, or an isolated hike in the mountains.

It is constructive, beneficial and prudent. Catastrophizing, on the other hand, seldom comes with a constructive and appropriate effort to prepare for future outcomes.

Speaking generally, catastrophic thinking as a form of prudent preparedness only makes sense when catastrophe is a realistic consideration. Catastrophizing NST is not like this; it is an inappropriate response to a small cue or event that leads to negative mental and emotional states.

In everyday situations, catastrophizing is based on inappropriate and unreasonable assumptions about future outcomes — an overreaction to some small event that spells disaster for the rest of the day. If you realize that this is happening, you could ask yourself why you choose to assume the worst would happen when it would be just as reasonable to assume the best outcomes? Most people would answer that avoiding disaster is worth anticipating, even when it doesn't happen.

Unfortunately, people tend to catastrophize because the human brain evolved to be very good at it. Catastrophizing is an important evolutionary advantage because it helps us recognize that the rustling in the bushes next to us on the path could be a dangerous predator, so we should run and save ourselves. This means that we always survive, even when we are wrong. That is why catastrophizing is hard-wired into our brains; humans have gained an evolutionary advantage from being able to anticipate danger and avoid it — at the cost of avoiding a 'danger' that wasn't really present in the first place.

In people with toxic habits of self-talk who constantly catastrophize every little thing, they tend to have way too much anxiety and hopelessness about the future than is healthy; they may also begin to believe that they will always be victimized by the next situation...

If you always think the worst is going to happen, then you will likely avoid taking simple risks, and you will tend to exaggerate situations and events in your life as being very negative when they simply aren't at all. This puts you in a state of chronic tension, anxiety, and stress, which can really impact your physical and mental health over time, not to mention prevent you from taking the amazing opportunities that life constantly throws your way. On the other hand, people who feel that life is abundant and supportive and filled with challenge and opportunity tend to be more successful and fulfilled — they also tend to see themselves in a much more dynamic and powerful way, one where they actually do have a decisive say in the events that happen in their own lives.

Feeling like you have opportunity in your life goes a long way to feeling good about your life and your achievements and positively affecting your daily motivation and happiness. By preventing catastrophizing negative self-talk, you won't unrealistically feel the dramatic victim of life's unforeseen circumstances.

If you detect catastrophic self-talk within you, then you can challenge those thoughts and really ask yourself, "How likely is it that? Really, how likely is it that these terrible outcomes will definitely happen?" Instead of feeling like the worst is definitely going to happen, you can be open and ready for what actually does happen. You can allow life to surprise you with how supportive it can actually be; how abundance can flow into your life if only you give it a chance to enter.

Try to consider how likely your assumed catastrophes actually are. Try to consider other outcomes instead; more reasonable expectations based on your real past experience, not your fears about the worst-case scenario. Being stuck in traffic, being paid late, people not calling you, not getting that job, not having good luck, these things might not mean the 'end of the world,' in fact, they usually don't mean that, far from it.

Catastrophes are extreme and are usually very unlikely — we shouldn't really be expecting them to happen very much at all unless your job is to plan for them explicitly. However, slightly uncomfortable mini-challenges are quite common and not such a big deal if you aren't disconsolate and demotivated because you assumed the worst.

The trick is to be mindful enough to catch this habit and nip it in the bud because unreasonable catastrophizing is harmful to your sense of self-worth, power, and personal feelings of agency. Even if the worst does happen, won't you be alright in the long run? Usually, the answer to this is "yes"; if you realize that fact at the moment, it can be a big relief. Taking a step back and checking in with reality can really help keep your stress down, which will help you make clearer decisions and meet the world head-on.

Negative Filtering

"I only notice the truth — the negative truth, of course, because I'm such a realist!"

Filtering, as the name implies, just means filtering out (ignoring) most positive aspects of a situation, person, or event in favor of a biased lopsided view, viz. your own negative view.

Catastrophizing is really a form of filtering, as is personalization, as are all the other types of negative self-talk. This is the case because to believe the unreasonable and repetitive negative self-talk, we have to ignore crucial facts about ourselves and the world; positive facts. We could not really believe our own NST while facing the truth of the world.

Negative self-talk is a learned conditioned habit of mind that we have fallen into - it is not rational behavior. Most of us know that it isn't rational. The irrationality of NST is not really the issue. The habit of doing it is an issue, and it can be very difficult to break.

Catastrophizing the future is different from describing the present negatively while ignoring all the present positive aspects. Filtering is about not paying attention to the positive aspects of the present moment and emphasizing and paying attention to the negative aspects. An everyday example of filtering is when you have a goal to save X amount of money per month, and you manage to only save 90% of your target amount. Instead of being proud of managing to save 90% of your target amount, you focus on that missing 10%. Guilty of filtering might judge themselves as useless, as they do not achieve their own goals or fulfill their own promises. Judging yourself for going over budget completely ignores (filters out) the fact that you did manage to save a significant sum of money in the first place — which could be cause for some pride in oneself.

Filtering is choosing to see the glass as half empty, lacking, missing half of what is needed. Filtering means that you approach things negatively instead of recognizing the objective fact that the negative aspects might only be a tiny fraction of the whole truth.

Thinking that contextualizes events negatively is just the same as framing the glass as half empty instead of half full. Positively framed (half full) thinking is beneficial and contributes to longevity, better health, sustained motivation, and better psychological outcomes. 'Half-empty' thinking that frames situations and events past or present negatively have been shown time and again to be self-defeating, biologically harmful, and psychologically damaging.

People who negatively filter their assessments of situations tend to judge their 'failures' as more important than their little successes. The truth is that most major achievements are accomplished in small daily increments (little daily `wins'), not one massive effort. Recognizing that the small 'wins' guarantee the big one's help you to realize that your efforts really matter — setting your sights on the daily tasks at hand helps you to see the true value of what you are doing day-to-day, rather than judging yourself when you fall short of unrealistic expectations.

People who negatively filter obsess over their imperfections or their perceived 'failures' are often perfectionists. You find yourself filtering, or feeling like nothing is going right, or devaluing yourself because you couldn't manage to reach your lofty ideals. It can help a lot to remind yourself of all the things that have actually gone right recently.

Bring back to conscious awareness that you filter out, and your tendency to become discouraged or feel like a failure becomes less and less each day because you gather the correct perspective and context for the events and situations in your life. Writing down the things that have gone right for you recently is a good way to attack this negative tendency head-on.

Overgeneralization

"I will never be able to...because this one time..."

Overgeneralization is when we expect negative circumstances in the present to keep happening over and over again in the future. It is a form of exaggerating negatively. For example, imagine you apply for a job, and your application is rejected. If you then say to yourself, "I'll never get a job, see, I didn't even get this one!" then you assume that the specific negative case happening right now will keep happening — "why even bother applying for jobs anymore, I'll just get turned down."

A similar scenario often happens to people when they attempt to ask someone out on a romantic date...if rejection leads you to conclude that you will never find a romantic partner, you have over-generalized this one failure. The same can be said for ordering food at a restaurant, and it arrives cold, "I always get the worst luck at restaurants!"

Magnification

"I can't remember names at a party....that proves my memory is bad...now I don't even try, what's the point? My memory is bad..."

Magnification is exaggerating your own flaws or errors. This can be a bit like catastrophizing because we can take small personal problems or qualities or events and blow them out of proportion by thinking they lead to disastrous outcomes.

Minimization

"You think I did great, but actually, I should have done better; just look at this little mistake. Obviously, I'm not so great!"

This is the opposite of magnification and happens when you ignore, minimize, or deny your positive qualities completely. This prevents you from taking pride in your own strengths and can land you in a negative cycle of feeling inferior and worthless. Good examples of minimizing include:

You cook an amazing meal, but you obsess over the fact that the rice was ever so slightly overcooked — making you think the meal was terrible or that you could have done better.

You play an amazing tennis match and win after a titanic struggle on the tennis court, but you criticize yourself because you should have done better.

Emotional reasoning

"You're a horrible person every time I have a bad day."

Using emotions in the present moment to guide what you decide to do can lead people to avoid discomfort and unpleasant emotional states. This can lead to procrastination and depression. People who exert effort and experience some discomfort in pursuing their most cherished goals tend to have a deep sense of fulfillment, but people who orient their actions based on emotional reasoning will tend to avoid making that effort because it is unpleasant in the immediate moment. Some examples include:

I'm not going to do my maths homework today; I really don't feel up to it.

If I was more motivated, I would enjoy my training, but I'm not, so I'm not going to train.

Fortune telling

'Why does the worst always happen to me?"

Fortune telling is like overgeneralization because it involves predicting a negative outcome in the future based on what happened in the present — except that in both cases there isn't much evidence to support our conclusion. Overgeneralization is more exaggerated than fortune telling, which is usually contained to the outcome of a specific event. Good examples include:

After writing an exam, we assume we did poorly even when we aren't sure.

After going to a job interview, you assume that they didn't like you because you were 'mind-reading' and then 'tell your fortune' by saying there's no way you got the job because they clearly didn't like you.

Learn To Filter Negative Thoughts

Has it ever happened that you had a certain experience, and while it wasn't all that bad, you could see no good in it? All you focused on were its negatives and magnified them to a huge extent?

For instance, you may have gone to a job interview and did your very best, but for some reason, you only remember one question that you felt you did not answer well, or how maybe your papers fell on the floor during the interview.

Negative filtering makes you disregard everything positively associated with an experience and worry only about the unpleasant details. Let us learn more about this thought process and how to overcome it.

Negative Filtering Distorts Your Thought Process

We consciously or unconsciously engage in negative filtering quite often, when you filter out all the positive information and aspects associated with an experience and focus only on the negative aspects. You discount the good parts and pick up the unpleasant ones only. If you generally get "A's" on all your test papers but get a "B" once, you disregard all the "A's" you have gotten so far and criticize yourself on that one "B". You chide and chastise yourself on and on.

Similarly, suppose you run a home bakery and deliver a cake to a client who likes it but points out a flaw. In that case, you fixate on that one mistake and completely ignore all the other things that were appreciated.

Negative filtering is mostly associated with extremely high and unrealistic expectations. These involve anticipating doing everything perfectly well.

Perfectionism is the standard against which you judge your efforts. If you meet it, you feel good about yourself. However, if you fall short of achieving it, you lament over the issue and criticize yourself. The truth is; nothing is perfect. There is always something that can be done better, something that can be improved on. Every time you chase perfectionism, you identify an area of improvement, which only triggers negative filtering.

To let go of excessive thinking, you have to overcome negative filtering. If you constantly fixate on the negatives associated with a situation, you stress yourself over trivial issues. Plus, you only hold on to the negatives and completely ignore all the positives associated with that experience. If you burnt the cake a little while baking it, you only worry about the burnt part, completely ignoring that you baked a whole cake for the first time. If you design your own website from scratch with a few errors, you belittle yourself for those mistakes without accepting that you made a website from scratch for the first time.

Negative filtering traps you into a barrage of unpleasant thoughts. Your vision narrows down, and you can see only one or two negative outcomes. Research by Barbara Fredrickson shows that negative thoughts narrow your horizon because you cannot see another outcome, but the worst-case scenario you have played in your head. This makes you nurture a negative state of mind that only makes you focus on the worst outcomes.

When you are sure only bad things will happen to you, the following problems take place:

- You stop trying harder to improve on your mistakes
- You don't get back up after faltering once
- You doubt yourself and your capabilities
- You are certain you are doomed for life
- You feel certain that only bad things will happen to you
- You feel agitated and grumpy almost always
- You settle for mediocre things, and often for those below your standards because you believe you don't deserve any better
- You let others treat you harshly and with disrespect

- You don't strive for excellence and miss out on opportunities for growth and improvement.

All these issues only disrupt your life quality and keep you from living a happy, well-rounded life. You certainly wish to improve on these problems, right?

In that case, here is what you can do to overcome negative filtering. Remember that many of these techniques can be applied to all sorts of negative thought processes so implement them every time you experience a bout of negative thinking.

Calm Yourself Down

When you feel a surge of stress mount inside you, and your breath becomes rapid and shallow from calm and placid, it is a sign you are thinking negatively.

At this moment, take slow, deep breaths. The square breathing pattern is an excellent technique to calm yourself gradually and relax. Here is how to do that:

Inhale through your nose to a count of 4 or 5. Focus only on inhaling and watch your in-breath as you breathe in. Notice any sensations you can sense in your body.

Hold that breath to a count of 4 or 5 and observe your bodily sensations during this time.

Slowly exhale to another count of 4 or 5 through your mouth this time. Stay with your breath as you did before and observe it very slowly and calmly.

As you exhale, hold on to the experience to a final count of 4 or 5.

Repeat these steps about 5 times.

In about 4 to 5 minutes, you will feel much calmer and focused than before. Do this every time you stress over weird, minute details and become fixated on negative outcomes, and you will start thinking rationally within minutes.

Identify and Accept the Negative Thought Without Labeling it

Once you feel calmer, try to identify that one negative thought that is spewing venom inside you. If you feel upset, why is it that you feel that way?

Is it because you didn't do well in your exam? If that's the issue, what exactly did go wrong? Try to identify the exact root of the problem, and once you identify that one negative thought that is creating havoc inside you - have a dialogue with it.

For that, you must learn to accept the thought without putting a harsh label on it. We have a habit of labeling and judging everything. You feel angry, and you put a negative label on your anger.

You think you won't fulfill any client orders, and you judge yourself for it. If you judge and label a certain thought as negative, you exacerbate the issue instead of resolving it.

At this point, you need to act very calmly and patiently. Mindfully accept the negative thought and don't treat them as something bad. Embrace it as a part of you trying to convey a concern to you to handle it respectfully and address it effectively. Take a few deep breaths, write down that thought in your journal and say, 'I accept this thought as a part of me,' and then thank your mind for bringing it to your awareness.

You may feel some sort of bitterness at this point. Take another deep breath and imagine it exiting your system. Do this a couple of times, and you will feel better. Imagine having a softer tone and form, such as a white cloud or a pink, fluffy bunny. This instantly gives it a softer, more welcoming appeal and makes you nurture a softer feeling towards it. This helps you accept it happily and then engage in a dialogue with it.

Engage in a Dialogue With the Negative Thought and Challenge it

Once you have improved your perspective of the seemingly unpleasant thought, enter in a dialogue with it.

Very politely, accept the thought and first try to question it. You could ask yourself questions such as, 'How do I feel about this thought?' 'What is it trying to convey to me?' 'Why do I feel this way?' and so on.

Next, question the authenticity of that thought. If you feel you won't deliver a good order to your client and it will be rejected, is there proof to validate this statement? Has it ever happened before? If yes, how many times? For instance, if your last order did not end well, why was it so? The customer could be at fault too, or there could have been other factors involved that weren't in your control. If you were at fault, understand and accept that you are a human and bound to err at times.

Think about how you would comfort a good friend if they went through this situation. You would probably calm them down and offer a nice rebuttal to their negative viewpoint. Tackle your unpleasant belief the same way. So, what if you made mistakes in the past? That does not give you the right to declare that your future will be dark every time.

Once you start to have a conversation with yourself, build on it so you can steer it in a positive direction.

When you feel calmer than before and have accepted that it is okay to falter and make mistakes and that your negative thought is only a fabrication of your mind, replace it with a positive suggestion.

Look at the Positives and Find a Positive Replacement for the Unpleasant Thought

At this point, you will be more open to the idea of an unpleasant scenario having some positives attached to it. Now is the time you need to look for any positives associated with that seemingly unpleasant situation and positively replace your unhealthy viewpoint.

Ask yourself if there is anything positive associated with that situation. Your mind is designed to answer your questions precisely in the manner you ask them. If you ask yourself why you could not get a certain job, it will put forward 101 reasons to illustrate just that. However, if you ask yourself how you can get a good job, it will detail all the routes you should take to accomplish the goal. This is how the human mind functions. To make it work constructively, take advantage of it, and use it the right way. Instead of worrying about why you don't do things right, focus on the good aspects associated with an outcome. For instance, if you were rejected for a job, ask yourself, 'what did I learn from the experience?' instead of fixating on 'why I did not get the job?' or 'why am I a loser?'

Your mind will instantly point out a few good things associated with the experience. In this case, it can be things such as learning to communicate with industry experts, preparing for the job interview, facing your fears, and so on. These are all the things you have gained from experience. When you learn so much from a situation, it surely cannot be all bad.

When you start looking at a situation from a more positive aspect, it stops scaring you. At this point, go back to your unconstructive belief and shape it into something more positive. For instance, if you earlier thought, 'I can never establish my business because I have failed countless times before,' change it to something more realistically positive such as, 'I have surely learned a lot from my setbacks, and I am ready to give it one more try.' Failure happens in life, but it's no big deal. You will learn valuable lessons and get ready to try again!

Remember to chant this newly formed positive suggestion several times to imbed it in your head.

This is how it will settle inside and slowly shape a positive belief system.

Work on these guidelines every time you spot an unsettling thought that creates discomfort inside you. Within a little while, you will change it into something more constructive and will slowly do away with negative filtering for good.

Overcome Perfectionism

Perfectionism, as mentioned earlier, is closely associated with negative filtering. When you chase perfectionism, you overburden yourself with the need to do everything right. Since nothing is really perfect, you feel dismayed and perceive things from a negative lens when you cannot accomplish that. To become a positive thinker, so you make the most of your life and live happily, overcome this need to be perfect. The right replacement for this attitude is to start settling for *good enough*.

Good enough refers to something that fulfills most of the criteria associated with a goal you are trying to achieve. For instance, if you have to deliver a business plan to a client in 7 days and your goal is to do it on the 6th day but end up doing it right when the 8th day starts, it is still good enough. Of course, the results could have been better, your performance has room for improvement, but this does not change the fact that you did deliver the final product. The deliverable was slightly past the deadline, but you ended up completing it nonetheless, and this does account for acknowledgment and appreciation.

When you stop chasing perfectionism and opt for good enough results, you enjoy the following positive results:

- You free yourself of the incessant and overpowering need to do everything right.
- You embrace your flaws and find it easier to move past them.
- You seek improvement and excellence in a more comfortable environment.
- You stop lamenting over what could have been and focus more on making most of the present moment.
- You work harder at the moment, are conscious of your shortcomings, and make conscious efforts to achieve the desired results.
- You easily overcome analysis paralysis as you do not stress yourself over what could have been and how things won't go right.
- You take action in the here and now and move towards your end goal.

In this process, you become more self-assured and stop fearing worst-case scenarios.

You realize there is some good associated with everything that helps you push past your limits, take risks, and try new things. In this process, you better discover and understand yourself.

All these changes only lead to a healthy, happy life. Let us look at how you can overcome the need to seek perfectionism in everything you do.

When you start a task, write down the target you are trying to achieve. If you are working on a loon-word blog post, your target could be to complete it in 5 hours.

Next, plan how to carry out the task in detail. Break the task into different milestones, with every milestone having one or more deliverables to fulfill. For instance, the first 90 minutes could be dedicated to researching the topic, and the final deliverable of the process could be to have a good topic with enough data on it to produce a loon-word written piece.

For every deliverable, write down the fulfillment criteria to know what you are trying to achieve.

Also, write down how to execute each phase of the process to know what step to take.

Once you have planned a task in depth, choose an appropriate time to work on it if you cannot do it right away.

Start the task on the prescribed time and gradually work your way through it.

Monitor your performance throughout the process and stop once you have worked on a certain deliverable so you can analyze it in detail.

Analyze your performance in an unbiased manner, pointing out all the strengths and weaknesses.

Celebrate the fact that you at least completed it, even if you did not do it as well as you had hoped or got past the deadline, but at least you tried. Pat yourself on the back and offer words of encouragement. This motivates you to work harder on the next milestone and move forward.

If, at any point, you feel the need to criticize yourself or start unconsciously pointing out only the flaws while filtering the good points, take a deep breath and calm yourself down. Remind yourself of your commitment to think positively and shift your focus to the positives. Do this a couple of times, and you will surely get the hang of it.

You do not have to work on all these strategies all at once. Go easy on yourself and take one baby step at a time. Slowly, when you climb the ladder, you will gain pace and achieve a compound effect one step at a time.

How to Overcome Personalization

Personalization and blaming are two more negative thought processes that lead to excessive thinking. To become calm, positive, and focused, it is crucial to break and eliminate these unhealthy thought processes.

Personalization

Personalization is a distorted thought process wherein you believe that everything someone else does or says is a direct and personal reaction geared towards belittling them.

If you engage in personalization, you take everything personally, even if something is not directed towards you. No matter what anyone says, you think they are trying to ridicule you. If your friend rolled their eyes, you are sure they did it at you and start to nurture ill feelings for them. If your boss admonishes your entire team, you think the lashing is aimed at you.

Personalization paves the way for other negative thought processes and makes you overthink stuff for no good reason. Here are ways to counteract this unhealthy thinking pattern:

Understand and accept the fact that everyone is entitled to their opinion. If someone disagrees with you, they have all the rights to do that. You need to stop taking it personally.

Unless and until someone pinpoints a flaw in you, do not take their gestures as an indication of your incompetence. Do not focus too much on the gestures someone makes because people are often unsure of their body language. However, if someone gives you negative vibes, it is best to distance yourself from them.

Pay attention to your social circle, and if you are surrounded by people who constantly engage in negative thinking and practice personalization too often, detach yourself from them. Their negativity is likely rubbing off on you and messing up your life.

Understand that you shine a negative light on yourself because everyone else is busy minding their own lives. If you want to feel better, stop perceiving everything you do from a negative lens.

Blaming

Suppose you feel others are responsible for every problem you encounter and feel no guilt in blaming them for your troubles. In that case, it explains why you feel so pessimistic often.

Blaming is an unhealthy practice, one that is of extreme detriment to your well-being. Take full accountability for your actions and life because it is your life and believe it or not, you are actually steering it in a certain direction.

Every time you find yourself looking for someone to put certain blame on, be it for getting stuck in traffic or buying the wrong kind of shoes, play the scenario in your head when you made a certain decision. You had the right to act a certain way, and if you did what someone else asked you to, that is on you as well. Start taking full accountability for your actions, and you will realize you always have a choice to do things as you want. This helps you make decisions the way you want and take better charge of your life.

It is best to dedicate an entire journal to your journey of positive thinking. Record all your daily practices and tactics in it along with your performance, and track it regularly. This helps you better analyze your strengths and weaknesses and move forward towards growth.

Turning Your Negative Thoughts Into Positive Thinking

Negative thinking can begin a downward spiral -- we have all been through it at some point or another. Sooner or later, you have got to drag yourself up and adopt positivity. Positive thinking may be the cure-all that you want to begin down a more joyful path in life. Below are a few suggestions that will support you with this:

Know Your Thinking Style

Among the initial steps toward changing your unwanted thinking patterns, you should know precisely the way you believe at this time. By way of instance, if you generally see yourself as a complete failure or success in each circumstance, then you're engaging in "black-and-white" thinking. Other negative thinking patterns comprise leaping to conclusions, catastrophizing, and overgeneralization.

Unhelpful believing patterns vary in subtle ways; however, they all involve distortions of fact and irrational methods of looking at people and situations.

Remind Yourself to Think Positively Daily

With hard work, dedication, and strength, nothing is hopeless. Negative thinking is ordinary, but too frequently, it's damaging to the entire body, mind, and soul. Every time you get a negative idea, redirect it to a favorable station.

Find the positive from the negative. It will be challenging, but it becomes more comfortable with practice. In the long-term, you'll be relaxed more frequently and appreciate life a great deal more.

Start Reading Positive Quotes

Reading positive affirmations will help provide you with the motivation you require for your day. It is time to turn off the television and get reading. It'll raise the spirits and allow you to feel fuller and glowing. If you do not have a good book available, get online, and do a few Google searches, or drop by the library and also spend a while on one of the bookshelves there. You're sure to think of a slew of quotes that will assist you to feel much better. Simply get up and be more proactive. You'll be thankful for it.

Begin Meditating and Imagining a Character in Your Thoughts

Picturing a character in your mind helps you to feel relaxed and positive. Whenever you have an inner sense of serenity and bliss, then you're more conscious of your environment. Practicing meditation was proven to decrease anxiety, enhance calm, and improve mindfulness and happiness. Like anything, it requires continuous training to reap the full advantages. Envision a relaxing destination and transport yourself. You're going to be surprised with just how rewarding this is.

Remember to Do the Things You Prefer

When you start looking ahead to something, your brain stays proactive. You feel fully operational; thus, organize a day with things that provide you real joy and help you on your search to think favorably. Life is too short to do what it is that you're made to do. Skiing, traveling the world, run with the bulls -- do whatever you make a step beyond your comfort zone.

Believe You Could Change Your Ideas

From time-to-time, the belief is all that matters. As they say, you can do whatever you set your mind to. If you believe you cannot alter your thinking, then it is very likely you won't ever but, with a positive mindset, just about anything you can. Just feel that great things will occur, and things tend to fall right into place.

Do Not Forget That Nothing is Permanent

Nothing is irreversible -- that is one fact that nobody could undermine. Should you take some opportunity to digest it genuinely, it is a lot simpler to begin thinking positively. Nothing is set in stone, and you will focus on changing the things you're not pleased with. Whether it is your relationships, your health, your professional life -- there are things you can do now to become happier later on.

Adopt Positive and Negative

Sometimes, you've got to remind yourself that where there's darkness, there's also light. However hard we try, the simple truth is that we're likely to get some kind of negativity in our lives occasionally. Life is a mixed bag. Everybody has their own struggles, and many people come out unscathed on the opposite side. Just make sure you search for the good in each situation - perhaps you will be surprised.

Exercise Mindfulness

Mindfulness has its origins in meditation. It's the practice of detaching yourself from the thoughts and feelings and seeing them as an external observer.

During mindfulness coaching, you will learn how to see your ideas and feelings as things floating beyond you, that you're able to stop and watch, or allow to pass you by. Mindfulness will aim to control your emotional responses to situations by enabling the believing part of your mind to take over.

Exercise Dealing With Criticism

Along with cognitive restructuring, the other facet of CBT, which is occasionally useful, involves the "assertive protection of itself" as it's likely that some of the time folks will indeed be critical and judgmental towards you. You must be ready to deal with criticism and rejection.

This procedure is typically conducted in treatment with a pretended dialog between you and your therapist to grow your assertiveness and assertive answers to criticism. These abilities are then moved into the actual world through homework assignments.

Chapter 15: Letting Go of Anger

True enlightenment and mental peace can never be achieved if your mind is full of hatred and grudge; hence, you must understand how you can let go of your anger. This is easier said than done, but this step will provide you with some essential steps to assist you in the long run.

But, before we go into the steps themselves, we must first understand what anger really is.

How Do You Define Anger?

While there are many different definitions of anger, the most general answer would be that anger is a very natural, yet at times irrational, or unwanted type of emotion that people experience from time to time in their day-to-day lives.

Various experts in this particular field tend to describe anger as an emotion that exists to protect us and help us survive in situations where we think we have been wronged.

The triggers that make us angry are discussed in detail in the next section. Still, you should know that whenever we are deprived of basic human needs, such as food or sleep, we tend to get irritated and feel angry.

Exhaustion, stress, criticism, frustration are also various factors that come into play when talking about anger.

When we are parents and are raising children, it is almost impossible to avoid some of these situations, which ultimately leads us to be angry and reacting so that we shouldn't.

Controlling your anger when you are a parent isn't easy, but it is nothing impossible either.

What are the possible reasons for our anger?

You may be wondering what is causing you to be so angry. We can all think about the various times in our lives when we got angry about something. Sometimes we could justify the anger that we were expressing, but there are many times when the outburst is over. We can't justify or even understand how we were feeling. No matter which one it fits under, you may be curious about why you feel so angry.

There are actually a few different reasons you may feel so angry in your life and what would cause you to feel this way.

Anger is helping you to cope with pain

There are times when you will be hurt emotionally, mentally, and physically. You are likely to do different things to help you to deal with this pain. Most people often use anger to deal with the pain that they are feeling. Anger can help them to either hide the pain that they are dealing with, or it can be used to channel that feeling over to someone else. It is pretty standard that angry people will just lash out because it helps them let off steam.

Anger is commonly a way for them to let out any of the pain that they are feeling. Usually, this pain is temporary, and when you are dealing with many problems in your life, it is not a surprise when you respond with a lot of anger. It can be a really cathartic release for people to use this anger, but there are many better and healthier ways to do this.

Anger can be your interpretation of things

People interpret the things that go on around them in many different ways. When people experience something and think it is unpleasant, it will often invoke an angry response. From this point, it is now up to the person to determine how they will express that emotion. There are different ways to express a person's anger. Still, the way that you react will depend on the way that you interpret a situation.

Anger can help you to get even

Some people may have gone through a bad experience in the past. Some people are still going through those bad experiences today. To help them deal with these unpleasant times, they always resort to directing their anger towards another person. Their anger is often triggered because they want to get revenge. Sometimes this revenge is rightfully aimed at the one they believe caused their pain, but sometimes it is not.

Those who have dealt with negative experiences in the past, whether it is hardship, failures, or abuse, are the kind of people who are more prone to anger issues and need anger management to deal with it at some point. This anger may have been triggered because of how this person is reacting to it now.

Anger is a way to hide vulnerabilities and emotions

Some people try to conceal their emotions for one reason or another. Some do it because they are trying to hide who they really are from other people. Others may do this because they want to mask their own weaknesses. No matter the reason, anger is often an emotion that shows others strength and will mask their insecurities. These people will always prefer to respond with hostility as they think it will help protect them against others who may harm them.

Anger helps them to justify wrong acts

Anger is sometimes used as an alibi to justify the wrongs that they may be doing. These people will go and do wrong or inappropriate things, and then they will say that they only did that because they were angry at the time. On paper, they have an excellent excuse to get them out of taking any responsibility for all the things they've done. This will only start a habit of always acting violently. Whenever someone calls them out on it, they can write it off later with anger as their excuse.

Think about how many times you have heard the phrase, "I did what I did because they made me angry." Anger helps you to feel righteous and makes you think you are morally superior to the other person. Still, it makes it hard to hold onto responsibilities for your actions.

As you have already seen, anger is never a result of complete spontaneity. It is usually rooted in something deeper. No matter what reason you have for the anger, most likely it was born out of an issue that you did not take the time to deal with when it was present.

Being able to address the reasons for your anger is at the heart of the principles and techniques used in most anger management programs. This is why it is so important for you to take some time to find the causes or reasons why you specifically get mad and the ways that you respond to it. This is a way that can make it much easier for you to manage your rage and manage the negative effects that cause you to feel angry all the time.

How do we express our anger?

One does not need to be a master of psychology to know that there are some real and serious effects of having too much anger in your life, especially if you are feeling angry all of the time. You simply have to reflect on some of your lifetimes when you have been angry and then see how you dealt with the situation. Every time you were angry, it is likely that you reacted in a way that surprised even you and in a way that is hard to justify in other situations.

There are some moments in your life when your anger will make you behave in a way that is completely different from how you usually are. It is not something that you necessarily need to beat yourself up about. Anger is something that everyone has dealt with at some point. However, assessing the causes and learning how to deal with them so that anger doesn't get the best of you is the best way to ensure that you achieve some great results in your attempts to overcome how much anger affects you.

There are a lot of different ways that people express their anger. Sometimes they will express it consciously and sometimes unconsciously. Here are a few of the ways that people will often choose to express their emotional anguish:

Some would suppress it

Some people will feel angry, but it cannot be seen just by looking at them. They will not express this anger because they are completely aware that something bad could happen if they decide to let it out. This will cause them to just keep the anger pent up inside.

While it is admirable that these people can control themselves so well when it comes to their anger, not expressing their rage can expose them to certain risks. Unexpressed rage and anger can sometimes lead to some health problems. It can also lead to the development of bad habits and behavior. Some think that it is a compromise, and they will keep it bottled up as much as possible, but such practices can also lead to other problems for some people.

Some prefer expressing the anger physically

Inflicting pain on yourself or on others is one of the frightening characteristics of poorly managed anger. Physical aggression falls into two main categories: aggression against people and aggression against objects. When it comes to aggression against other people, this kind of aggression involves inflicting physical harm, such as doing it with your own hands or using weapons. Still, it is not limited to things like pushing, slapping, and punching.

There is also anger which is aimed at objects, and it is usually random. This can include slamming doors, banging walls, and throwing random objects. Physical expressions of anger will often cause obvious damage and can be traumatic for anyone who witnesses or experiences it.

Some prefer to express verbally

There is a lot you have probably heard about the physical aspect of anger. Still, verbal abuse can also occur, and it is often very destructive as a form of anger manifestation. People verbally express their anger in other ways, and this can cause a lot of hurtful effects.

Using this way to express their anger may raise their voice, insult others, threaten, embarrass, or use profanity. Verbal abuse is sometimes a one-time event, but there are many cases where an event of verbal abuse will repeat itself over a longer period. When it is expressed verbally, anger can inflict lasting damage to the one who receives it.

Some prefer to express indirectly

Some people will work to make sure that they are not expressing their anger directly. Some do it out of fear that they are mad or don't want to get angry because they know it makes them look bad. This is why they may want to consider indirectly expressing their anger.

There are many ways that indirect aggression shows itself, which includes actions, such as purposeful ignoring, dismissiveness, and angry stares. Some will go with an action that is more passive-aggressive and will include negative body language, purposely doing tasks poorly, or sulking. At times, they may want to confide their frustrations to others as a substitute for dealing with their anger directly.

Some prefer to express anger at others

Displaced anger is sometimes a common way to express anger. You can always see this form of expressing anger no matter where you are. People can't always express their anger to something or someone at the moment that it happens.

Instead of showing the anger to the right person, they will choose to vent it to someone else. Often, this will be another person who just happened to be close by. This can include friends, subordinates at work, or even children. Displaced anger manifests itself in many ways at work.

Some will change their behavior

Anger is an emotion that can completely shape the way a certain person will act in various situations. In response to anger, some will undergo several changes in their personality or behavior. Some of these changes will subside once the feelings of anger start to go away, but some changes might stick around for a longer period.

The biggest behavioral change that you can observe in an angry person is that they seem to become more aggressive in their behavior, which can come in the way of more illogical thoughts and actions. Some may build up walls of bad feelings and resentment, making it difficult for others to reach out to them. Some will avoid others to deflect the bad feelings. There will be some situations where this anger is actually beneficial to you, but most of the time, it will only negatively affect everyone involved. And when that anger sticks around for a long time, it can only cause more harm than good in the long run.

Looking at the common triggers of anger

What makes an individual angry varies from one person to the next. What is a trigger for you might not be a trigger for someone else whom you know. Being a parent is already hard. With kids always messing everything up, it is normal for these triggers to get amplified and explode unfavorably. A key to bringing your anger under control is to understand what your anger triggers are.

Below is a breakdown of the most common triggers of anger that you should know about:

People related

- Loud people all around you
- Someone you know not paying you back
- Messy/rude neighbors of room mates
- People making insensitive jokes about topics you favor
- People asking various rude questions or just being nosy

Places related

- Unfavorable work environment
- Crowdy stores
- Crowdy public transport
- Excess traffic
- Waiting a long time in lines
- Places that might make you feel like you are suffocating
- Places that might bring up bad memories

Situations related

- Where you are feeling hungry, exhausted, or lonely
- A situation where you are wrongly accused of something

- Having to clean up someone else's mess
- Having to hear hurtful rumors or gossip
- Having something stolen from you

And so on.

Now obviously, yours will vary, but this list is written to give you a general idea of what might trigger you to get angry in the first place. The idea is to identify them and tame them so that they don't take you over.

The Benefits Of Letting Go Of Anger

Anger management strives to reduce and manage the emotional and physiological triggers, which incite anger. At times, you cannot get rid of change or avoid certain things, people, or circumstances that trigger your anger, but you can certainly control how you react. One thing you will always have absolute control over regardless of the circumstances is the way you choose to respond. In this section, you will learn about the different benefits that anger management offers.

Empathy quotient

Anger management helps improve your empathy towards others and, in turn, this helps you understand other people's perspectives. Usually, anger tends to escalate because people fail to see a situation from another person's perspective. Once you start becoming more empathetic, instead of thinking about everything from your perspective, you become more considerate towards other people's perspectives too. If you can do this, then it reduces the chances of a conflict. Also, empathy is a brilliant trait, which will come in handy in all aspects of your life.

Better relationships

Usually, most people tend to avoid their loved ones when they realize that their anger can hurt others. Since your closest circle consists of people you love, they often become the unintended victims of your angry outbursts. By learning to control your emotions, it makes it easier to develop healthier and happier relationships.

Anger management gives you a chance to learn about your anger, its triggers, and its causes. The way that you feel and behave is directly related to what you feel and experience. By becoming aware of your emotions, you can easily understand what prompts them. For instance, you might realize that your anger is usually because of some repressed guilt or sadness you feel. Often, anger cloaks certain underlying emotions. So, anger management gives you an insight into your feelings and emotions. Once you understand all this, it certainly becomes easier to control and manage.

Better judgment

Does a fight with your loved one make it difficult to concentrate on your work? Well, anger can cloud your judgment. When you are angry, rational and logical thoughts tend to go out of the window, and instead, anger tends to govern the way you react and behave. When your anger is under control and you are calm, you can think clearly and make better decisions. Anger management will help control your emotions, and this, in turn, will improve your decision-making skills.

A significant benefit of anger management is the ability to manage stress. When your stress levels decrease, you will notice that it becomes easier to avoid any anger triggers and stay in control of any situation. Less stress also means better health. Apart from this, it improves your efficiency and productivity, so by learning to manage your anger, you can effectively reduce your stress levels.

Avoid aggressive communication

Anger is quite a powerful emotion, and it often triggers aggression. If you can communicate effectively and efficiently, then you can easily avoid any angry outbursts. A lot of problems can be solved rather easily if you can communicate efficiently. By communicating this way, you can reduce miscommunication and express yourself clearly. Instead of responding aggressively, when you learn to manage your anger, you will assert yourself properly. Anger management will help you understand that you can effectively assert yourself without aggression.

Understand your responsibility

Anger management will help you understand and recognize the ways you are responsible for your anger. It helps you become aware of your anger, along with the reasons for it. A combination of these factors will help regulate and manage your anger.

Now that you are aware of all the different benefits of anger management, it is time to learn more about the steps involved in this process.

Learning to Identify the Causes of Anger

You may be wondering what is causing you to be so angry. We can all think about the various times in our lives when we got angry about something. Sometimes we could justify the anger that we were expressing, but there are many times when the outburst is over. We can't justify or even understand how we were feeling. No matter which one it fits under, you may be curious about why you feel so angry.

There are actually a few different reasons you may feel so angry in your life and what would cause you to feel this way.

Anger is helping you to cope with pain

There are times when you will be hurt emotionally, mentally, and physically. You are likely to do different things to help you to deal with this pain. Most people often use anger to deal with the pain that they are feeling. Anger can help them to either hide the pain that they are dealing with, or it can be used to channel that feeling over to someone else. Commonly, angry people will just lash out because it helps them let off steam.

Anger is commonly a way for them to let out any of the pain that they are feeling. Usually, this pain is temporary, and when you are dealing with many problems in your life, it is not a surprise when you respond with a lot of anger. It can be a really cathartic release for people to use this anger, but there are many better and healthier ways to do this.

Anger can be your interpretation of things

People interpret the things that go on around them in many different ways. When people experience something and think it is unpleasant, it will often invoke an angry response. From this point, it is now up to the person to determine how they will express that emotion. There are different ways to express a person's anger. Still, the way that you react will depend on the way that you interpret a situation.

Anger is a way to hide vulnerabilities and emotions

Some people try to conceal their emotions for one reason or another. Some do it because they are trying to hide who they really are from other people. Others may do this because they want to mask their own weaknesses. No matter the reason, anger is often an emotion that shows others strength and will mask their insecurities. These people will always prefer to respond with hostility as they think it will help protect them against others who may harm them.

The Importance of Breaking the Cycle of Hatred

One big reason why many people are feeling a lot of anger is dealing with failed relationships. At some point in your life, you must have already dealt with a failed relationship, whether it is with a family member, friend, or someone else in your life. Some of these failures will hurt you more than others, and this means that they have the potential to drastically alter your attitude and perspective.

One of the best things you can do to help reduce the amount of anger you are feeling is to resolve this issue and prevent frustrating and problematic relationships. If you really want to have a happy life, you need to break this endless cycle. Let's take a look at some of the steps you can take to help you make this happen:

Change your attitude

There are times when the problematic relationship is caused by you. It is either you choose to stay with that bad relationship, even when you should leave, or you are the one who is making it toxic but can't seem to see it or understand why. So, you first need to assess whether you are the problem or not. There are times when it is your resolve to stay with that relationship that is frustrating.

Now, there are times when the other person is causing the issues in the relationship, but it could simply be you who is the reason for the issues. Suppose you are in a toxic relationship because you want to be better than the other person or think you have to. In that case, it is time to get out of it and make yourself recover. The frustration comes from you in this scenario.

Try to be more kind

You will find that being kind is one of the most valuable things you can do when you want good, lasting relationships. People are naturally drawn towards kind people. Think of the kind of people you want to hang out with, the ones who are the most attractive to you. Do you want to spend your day with someone who is happy, kind, and outgoing, or do you want to spend your time with someone who is angry and mean all the time? You will likely choose to go with the former, and you should strive to become a person like that.

You can also use this to your advantage. When you treat people kindly, they return the favor and treat you in the same way. This kindness you received will give you a positive vibe throughout the day, which will leave less space for bitterness and anger to grow. It does not matter how others treat you; you must show kindness each day.

A good place to start is to smile more often. This does not take a lot of effort on your part, and it will give you a huge payoff. You should also be thankful and appreciative of all the things you have in your life, such as the material wealth you possess and those who value you. Take some time to compliment and help others each day. These are just a few of the things that you can do to be kind to those around you.

Stop trying to get even

Whenever you are stuck in a cycle of having bad relationships, it feels tempting to get even with the other person. When you feel that they have wronged you, you will likely want to get revenge on them. You do not need to live life like this and feel like you need to retaliate against those who have done wrong to you. The desire to get even will reflect on the way that you treat others. It is a lot of energy that you are taking away from your progress and the happiness you are looking for in life.

This means that if you want to break this cycle and start to maintain more meaningful relationships, it is time to break away from that desire to get even with others. You need to learn how to forgive others, as well as learn how to forgive yourself. Accept that you have been hurt and that you are hurting, and then look for some ways to resolve these feelings before moving on.

Make sure to filter your relations

When it is time to break that cycle of bad relationships, it means that it is a good idea to pick out the right relationships to pursue from the start. It doesn't really matter what your intentions were in the beginning. If you keep choosing bad relationships, then obviously they will end up badly. You may be surprised to find out that you may have subconsciously entered into these bad relationships. This can include relationships where you care for people who do not care for you or ones where you get attached to those who have trust issues. It is just a fact that some people are looking for love in the wrong place.

Suppose you would like to break out of this bad cycle with relationships. In that case, it is important to choose the right relationship wisely from the beginning. This is sometimes hard to deal with initially, but it can help you avoid some heartache and a lot of anger and frustration in the future.

Understand that communication from both sides is important

No matter what kind of relationship you are in, it is important to be a two-way street. For these relationships to thrive, both sides need to be willing and able to make things work. Now, there is always more than one way where both sides can find a middle ground that will benefit each of them. Sometimes you may have to give a little bit more than the other person. But if you are the only one who is giving, and the other person never gives anything, then this is definitely a relationship that will only leave you frustrated.

First, you must make sure that your lines of communication are open at all times. You need to speak your mind and share that with the other person, but you should always listen to what the other person says. Both sides need to make it a priority to build up some mutual trust. You and the other person in that particular relationship should make it an effort to make each other better, to create an environment where the whole is greater than the sum of its parts. When you can effectively do this, it will lead to a much better relationship. Much of the anger and frustration you are experiencing is tied to your inability to create and maintain healthy relationships. As such, it is a given that when you are trying to manage the excess anger that you are dealing with, you will need to also learn how to manage many of your relationships as well. It will not cure all of the problems you have, but it can help make your life better and help make it easier to work on your anger in other parts of your life.

The Importance of Emotional Intelligence and Forgiveness

Emotional intelligence, otherwise known as emotional quotient, can identify and control your emotions and those close to you. It is argued that for you to be emotionally intelligent, you need to have at least three primary skills:

Managing emotions

You need to know and understand how to guard yourself against getting an emotional breakdown that can lead to fury. This includes regulating your emotions and those that others may have too.

Emotional awareness

This is a state of naming or identifying your emotions based on how you view them.

Harnessing emotions

You should also harness your emotions and redirect them to other tasks, such as problem-solving.

Unlike the general intelligence factor, emotional intelligence doesn't have a particular test or scale used to measure it in a person. This has led to the argument by many psychologists that emotional intelligence is not an actual construct. They argue that it is only a way to gauge interpersonal skills from one person to the next. Despite the many critics, EI (Emotional Intelligence) appeals to the wider majority in society. This has gone further into the corporate world, where prospective employees use it in their job applications. This is through the attachment of emotional intelligence tests taken to prove better leadership skills.

While some research studies find a correlation between emotional intelligence and job performance, others fail to identify any relationship of the sort. The absence of scientifically-backed tests makes this situation even worse than it is since it is almost impossible to gauge the contribution that EI has on job performance.

It is quite straightforward to know someone who is emotionally intelligent. Such people tend to be aware of their states, whether having positive emotions or negative ones. Again, they can control either from getting out of hand. Such people can bear with frustration, anger, and sadness, among many other emotions, without breaking down. They can also prevent the other person from having an outburst, especially when there is an argument or conflict. They can also help to reduce sadness and anxiety in someone else through what they say or do. They, therefore, tune themselves into the emotions of others, thus getting to understand how to treat or handle them.

When you are emotionally intelligent, you will not easily vent your frustrations and dissatisfaction to the next person close to you and channel your emotions to the right places. Emotionally intelligent people have a lesser likelihood to erupt during arguments or when disappointed.

Anger and emotional intelligence

Anger is a potent emotion with negative consequences on the person facing it and the people around. When you are prone to it, people will be distant from you as they will not know your next reaction. However, bottling up your anger is equally a tragedy awaiting as you will ultimately blow up after reaching the peak in your frustrations. Therefore, the ideal way to handle anger is not to ignore it but to deal with it. People with frequent anger outbursts often regret it at the end of the day because they take things out of proportion in most cases.

When you are emotionally intelligent, it is easier for you to understand or recognize different emotions. After that, you can use the information you understand to make a decision. This is a skill that greatly helps in dealing with anger. It also helps you understand that you need to choose your battles instead of seriously taking every one of them.

The absence of emotional intelligence in a person creates many problems, aside from anger management troubles. It can affect your ability to recover from different emotions, such as sadness and a difficulty understanding other people. Here are a few ways in which emotional intelligence helps with anger:

It helps you to control your thoughts

You may not have much control over a situation taking place, but you can control what you think about it. You can adjust your mind to think in a certain direction that is healthier and safer for you and the other person. Focusing on your thoughts can help you control your emotions to some extent.

There is one brilliant quote to help you digest this idea better - you can't prevent a bird from landing on top of your head, but you can prevent it from building a nest and living there. Take the bird as your emotions. Through your thoughts, you can prevent your emotions from taking the better part of you and prevent yourself from being a slave to your feelings. You should be the one controlling your emotions and not the other way around.

Helps you to take feedback and criticism

Criticism isn't always a bad thing. At times, it can help you become a better person and correct your flaws, if any. The only disadvantage of criticism is when it is negative. Nobody appreciates negative criticism that often irritates and agitates. It is quite easy to get mad at someone negatively criticizing you, especially when they put it in a way that isn't palatable and respectful. But when you employ emotional intelligence, you will understand that this is a chance to learn even if delivered inappropriately. It also helps you know how others reason and think, which can form the basis for decision-making.

When next somebody gives you a negative criticism, try to learn their perspective and look at how it can make you a better individual.

Helps you understand your feelings and emotions

Emotional intelligence helps you to understand yourself more and have the capabilities of recognizing your emotions or feelings. It also helps you understand the impact of these emotions or feelings on yourself and others. Understanding this alone will help you control your anger and regulate frequent outbursts. To understand your emotions, you must first sit back and reflect on different issues, including:

- What may influence the actions or words of others?
- How your moods may lead you to anger or affect your decisions.
- Personal emotional strengths and weaknesses.

Often a reflection on matters such as these can give you the needed insight for solving problems without anger.

Improves your empathy

Empathy involves showing high levels of understanding other people. This includes getting to know how they feel and what they think. Emotional intelligence can greatly influence this ability and help you understand others more. It will make you less judgmental and quick to labeling others by their thoughts, behaviors, and feelings. Instead, you will be willing to see things from their perspective and get why they do and say certain things.

Often people confuse empathy with plainly agreeing with what somebody else is saying; this is not the case. It is more like using their perspective to determine how you react to what they say or do. This helps you to be in sync with them and reduce any chances of misunderstanding. You will also be less prone to ire, even at the highest provocation. This is because you will set your mind to perceive things as per the other person's perspective and not your own. Empathy is seen as one of the best ways to build stronger relationships and ties between people. Sometimes it takes only one person to have empathy, and this will greatly reduce conflicts.

Allows you to praise others

When you are emotionally intelligent, you will understand that nothing sounds sweeter to a person's ear than their praises. Everyone loves to be praised for something they did or even just for the sake of it. It is an item that every human craves. Praises build trust and love between and among people. When you commend someone for a job well done or are disciplined, you make them have trust in you and reduce any negative approach.

To praise others needs you to be focused on their good side. Avoid being negative and only looking at the negative aspects of others. This often creates resentment and rebellion, which leaves you on the receiving end of the negative emotions. For instance, as a couple, you need to complement each other more often to reduce conflicts and anger outbursts. When you're always pointing out the negatives in your significant other, this will make them susceptible to anger. Remember that this is a feeling which emerges due to discontent and the idea that you are under attack from someone else, whether physically or emotionally. In this case, this is an emotional attack, and the aggrieved partner will want to fight back. Psychologists also say that you constantly motivate them to be their best versions when you share positive things that you appreciate about someone.

Teaches you to say sorry

The word sorry is a five-letter word that can make or break a relationship. People don't fancy apologies, mostly because they think it makes them the 'little' person. This is especially advanced by another three later words - ego. It takes courage and strength to say sorry. And as much as some may view it as a sign of weakness and defeat, it is the strongest display of courage from anyone. It also shows that you are humble and can retract your words for the sake of peace and friendship.

Saying sorry has a lot to do with emotional intelligence. A person who is not emotionally intelligent will rarely see the need to apologize in any situation. Sometimes you need to apologize even if you are on the right side. When dealing with a quick to anger person, you need to show them that you are the subject and are the ruler. This way, they can tone down their anger. There is no need for both of you to have sharp arguments, and nobody is willing to be the 'little' one; the debate will not end. Emotional intelligence will show you two things: apologizing doesn't make you a lesser person. It doesn't necessarily imply that you are the wrong individual. Instead, it means that you have placed more value on your relationship or friendship than your personal feelings and thoughts.

The importance of forgiveness

Whenever you decide to forgive, you are essentially making a conscious decision to give up any revenge thoughts. Are you wondering why you need to forgive? When you choose to forgive someone, you don't have to make excuses or access any wrongdoing, which has happened to you in your past. You don't have to forget any trauma you were subjected to necessarily. It is merely about letting go of any resentment. When you do this, you are essentially getting rid of any suppressed anger within. While you forgive someone, it is not necessary that you must try for reconciliation.

You might forgive someone, but you can also choose to end that relationship. It certainly helps improve your overall psychological well-being. When you're angry or have any resentment within, then revenge might seem like a good idea.

However, holding onto a grudge or plotting revenge is merely a waste of your time and will not do you any good. A lot of people seem to think that revenge will make them feel better. Wouldn't it be better if you could get even with someone who wronged you? Well, you might think that revenge will give you the satisfaction you desire. However, it will only make you feel worse.

It is quite easy to get sucked into any temptations about indulging or plotting revenge. It might be a fantasy that you like obsessing over. It might think that payback is the best way to get over any injustice or wrongdoing you think you faced. However, when all you do is think about revenge, you are essentially concentrating only on the hurdle of experience. The more time you spend thinking about your grievance, the worse it will get. Instead of finding a way to solve the problem on hand, if you concentrate on the hurt you suffered, it will only worsen your mood and make you feel dissatisfied. The longer you focus on the negative aspects, the longer it will take to find happiness. Also, if you're not careful, you can become quite obsessed with these negative thoughts.

Forgiveness is an act of generosity towards others as well as yourself. When you forgive someone, you're offering them a gift of compassion, even if what that person has done was wrong in the past.

However, you are also granting yourself compassion by forgiving. Forgiveness can help in forming better and healthier relationships. Apart from this, it also helps reduce any emotional stress you're experiencing. By learning to forgive, you can let go of your anger rather easily.

Learning to forgive

Anger and hate can be triggered rather easily; however, learning to forgive is an art. Forgiveness doesn't come naturally, and it takes a conscious effort. Once you decide to let go, you can free yourself from the unnecessary burden of blame, resentment, or anger. This process certainly takes a little effort, but it will be worth your while. You must understand that the art of forgiveness is not restricted to a single act, but it is an ongoing process. You cannot truly forgive yourself or others unless you come to terms with your anger. It certainly isn't easy to let go, especially when you know you are right and that you deserve justice, but it is always in your best interest to let go. The good news is you can learn to forgive. The following steps will help you start the process of Forgiveness:

Start by acknowledging your anger

You cannot forgive if you do not accept your anger, so you must make a conscious effort to understand, acknowledge, and accept any anger or pain you feel. Feel your anger as deep and intense as you can and connect the same with certain instances or transgressions committed against you. You cannot truly let go of your anger until you accept that your anger is present and real. Until you feel it and connect yourself with it, you cannot let go of it.

Forget about taking revenge

You cannot truly forgive anyone if you indulge yourself by thinking about possible revenge. If you want to move towards forgiveness, you need to stop plotting about revenge, regardless of how justified you think it is. If you are certain that you want to let go, you must make a conscious effort to stop thinking about revenge or punishment. Take a moment and think about it. How can you possibly ever move on if you keep going back to the same incident?

The other's perspective

When you're under the influence of anger, it is quite likely that you will think about things in an absolute manner. However, this sort of thinking that everything is either black or white isn't good. Black-and-white thinking leaves no room to think about all the shades of grey, which might have influenced the other person to act or behave in the manner that they did. Take a moment and forget about your anger for a while. Instead, try to think about things from the other's perspective. When you do this, you might understand why the other person acted the way they did. By taking a mental timeout and reframing your thoughts or looking at the situation objectively, you might better understand the situation. It might even allow you to be compassionate towards the other person. A combination of these things certainly makes it easier to grant forgiveness.

Know that there will be hurt

Yes, other people's words or deeds might have harmed you; however, remember that there is nothing that you can do today to change the past. Let the past stay where it belongs — in the past! Your past can be a learning experience for you, but you must not allow it to control your present.

You can always take the pain you have felt and then transfer it to the person who caused you the same pain. Well, this sounds rather petty and doesn't give any productive results. You are the only one who has the power to let go of your thoughts and anger.

The final step is to grant forgiveness once you go through the previous steps.

Deal With Your Emotional Burden and Let Go of Destructive Habits

Dealing with your past while being a parent isn't an easy task. However, there are certain steps that you can take to shoot down those negative emotions and become a better "you," and the primary one that I personally love is to practice positive thinking.

How to think positive

When you develop and improve positive thinking, it goes beyond just what you think about that makes you smile. It becomes your environment. It becomes who you are as an individual. Positivity - just like negativity - consumes us. It can be tough to think positively when you have a rough day or when everyone or everything around you seems depressing or worrisome. But the truth is when you think positively, your aura and mind stop looking for the bad in every situation, and you become grateful for these hard days and extreme failures because they shape your destiny. In every horrible scenario, there is good that you can take from it. At first, seeing the positive in situations can be very difficult, but it will become so easy that you won't even need to think; the positive will be there.

Before going to sleep at night, rehash your day in your mind. Think about everything that happened and take three positive perceptions away from the day. It could be anything. Was the sun shining? Did you reconnect with an old friend? Maybe your boss or co-worker wasn't that grumpy today, making you have a less stressful day. The more you start seeing the little positive effects, the more your perception of positivity will develop. The quicker happiness and success will come.

Try to do something nice for someone

It may not seem like it, but acts of kindness can lift your spirits and lift someone else's spirits. When we do something excellent for others, we feed our soul with positivity because those chemical endorphins shoot off in our brains as a reward response. These acts could be anything, such as smiling at a stranger, waving to a co-worker, or pausing to do something thoughtful for someone you know. When you make someone else smile, your heart smiles, making you feel better about yourself and developing confidence.

Learn to be in the present

If I haven't said this enough, then let me repeat it: Be mindful! Once we live in the moment, it creates balance and structure in our awareness of what is going on around us. When we become aware of our surroundings while staying in the present moment, we will be able to better pick up on the positive things that happen, and negativity will seem like a distant friend.

Practice self-love and gratitude

The thing about positivity is that when you love yourself, it becomes easier to help others and give back to the universe. Just think about it - if you don't love yourself, then your relationships fall apart faster, your job never seems to feel satisfying. You continuously second-guess your ability to handle stressful situations. However, when you love yourself, you can be thankful for what you have because you have it. You won't be asking for more or for things that you don't have, and envy or jealousy won't seem like important things to worry about anymore. Any chance you get be grateful for what you have, rather than envy what you don't have. The grass is rarely greener on the other side.

Changing your mood

Most of the time, we get stuck in negative thought patterns because our moods are dark. It's a cycle - negative or worrisome thoughts bring on bad moods, which bring on perceptions of more negative outcomes, making it hard to make crucial decisions because our minds are crowded, leading to overthinking (or negative thoughts) and so on. Some days we don't want to get out of bed, and other days we are motivated, which produces "feel good" chemicals that result in getting more done. So, on the days you feel down, stressed out, anxious, or depressed, think about the productive days and draw from that energy. Sometimes, it is okay to give in to your dark mood; try not to sulk or make it a daily habit.

Get more exercise

We talked about this already as well. When you work out, those "feel good" chemicals are released in your brain and instantly change your mood. It is also a good distraction from your bad mood because instead of focusing on what got you so upset, you can focus on other things, like the scenery or your breathing. Make sure to drink water while you work out, as being dehydrated can make you feel worse.

Try watching more inspiration and motivational contents

When you don't feel like moving or getting out of bed and watching an inspiring movie or listening to an uplifting podcast, you are having just one of those days. Even though we like to listen to music that matches what we feel in our down moments, ignore this urge and do the opposite - crank up some happy, upbeat tunes. Who knows, it may even want to make you dance or sing. It will lift your spirit 60% faster by listening to, or watching motivational material over listening to, or watching harmful, depressing material. Interestingly, when we listen to what suits our mood at the moment, we are training our brains that these attitudes are okay, and then we find ourselves falling deeper into the negative cycle.

Bring about a more positive body language

This means that you should act and behave the way you want to feel. So, if you want to feel confident, then prance around the house in the sexiest or wackiest thing that you have and pose in front of a mirror with your chest puffed out and your back straight. If you want to feel relaxed, then throw on your comfy clothes and lounge around, but be mindful of what you tell yourself. Force yourself to smile for 60 seconds, and I guarantee your mood will lift, even if only slightly. Don't let negativity consume you; break free by being you. Be funny, laugh, tickle yourself, talk to someone about your aspirations and dreams, or do whatever you need to get out of the funk you are in and into the mood you want to have.

Learn to appreciate the little things in life

Here is a weird, funny fact: We find it normal when someone goes around and complains about everything. We listen to our friends vent, our parents' bicker, our bosses complain, and even strangers arguing with themselves sometimes. It is "normal" to listen to someone complain and bicker about things, but wouldn't it be weird if we heard someone going off about how grateful and appreciative they are about everything? How typically do you hear an individual say, "It is raining outside, and I am so grateful for the rain," or, "Food is often taken for granted, so I just wanted to take a moment to feel blessed for this food." Have you ever heard someone say, "I appreciate that my kids scream and give me attitude because it means that they are growing human beings?" No, you probably haven't. Imagine if you said out loud everything you were grateful for today, everything you appreciated today and even yesterday. Just envision how you'd feel and what you'd make someone feel. You may even have a good laugh, but isn't that the point? Practice this.

Enforce positivity

The truth about your thoughts is that they do not control you. This is the same with moods; they don't control you. So, when you have a hard time practicing or enforcing the past techniques, do it anyway. Force yourself to smile, force yourself to get out of bed and dance, force yourself to feel grateful. Once you get up and force positivity in your day, you are taking control of your surroundings and your behavior. This teaches your brain that you control how you react to them, which creates positivity and healthy habits even in downtimes and dark moods.

Enforcing positive habits

Sometimes thinking positively and changing your mood isn't enough to develop a positive attitude regularly. You have to create habits so that your brain stops synapsing the negative enforcements you have created and starts synapsing the positive ones. While the past exercises will work for the short-term, you will need to practice these every day and create healthy daily habits. Suppose you stay consistent in creating positive habits. In that case, you will become less anxious, less of a "worrywart," and more easy-going. The minute you know you have succeeded in being positive, you stop feeling tense during the day. You see the light in all situations. You will feel clear-minded, and you will have acceptance of what you can't control, meaning you have acknowledged that negativity no longer consumes you as you have taken the control back.

Another interesting approach is the "Sedona Method."

Once you have become aware that a situation requires action, continuing to experience a negative emotion can become more of a hindrance than an aid. In fact, in many cases, the emotional imbalance becomes the greater problem. Let's learn how to eliminate negative emotions once their role is no longer helpful.

If you get upset when you have a problem, like most people, often you begin to think about how upset you are. Before you know it, the feelings of upset become a much bigger problem than the original situation that caused your unhappiness. Here is how most people try to deal with this problem.

Most people try to suppress negative emotions. They tell themselves, "I will not feel upset or unhappy anymore." It's so unfortunate that this is the worst thing you can do to eliminate negative emotions. You are strengthening it. Why? Your unconscious brain does not understand negative words. Let me prove this to you. Don't think about Mickey Mouse singing the national anthem. Don't think about eating pizza. Don't think about being upset. What happened? You immediately begin to think about whatever you tell yourself, "Don't think about..."

The last thing you want to do to eliminate a negative emotion is not to think about it. As you can see, this only makes it stronger. So what can you do to eliminate the problem? Think about the exact opposite of your problem. For example, if you are thinking about how nervous you are feeling, say to yourself, "I feel relaxed and at peace." Repeat this over and over again. Instead of trying to stop feeling a negative emotion, you want to create the positive emotion you want to experience. Creating a positive affirmation that is the opposite of your problem and repeating it repeatedly will eliminate your negative emotion. Try it, and you will be amazed at how easily you can overcome your problem.

The Sedona Method

An important step in creating wealth and creating your choice's life is to release any emotions that get in the way of attaining the things you want. The Sedona Method is a basic but effective, easy-to-learn technique that allows you to let go of any negative, unpleasant or painful feelings you can feel at any given time.

Trying to get ahead in life while feeling negative emotions such as anger, fear, or anxiety is like pushing your car's gas pedal while the handbrake is on. You may be able to move forward, but it will take an enormous amount of effort and energy, and you won't get very far. To reach your goals, you need to release the resistance, or the negative feelings, that have stopped you in the past.

The Sedona technique consists of a set of questions you ask yourself, which lead your awareness to concentrate on what you feel at the moment and subtly direct you into letting go of it. Unplugging negative emotions produces a shift so that your emotional energy can work for you instead of against you. Having better relationships, a more fulfilling and rewarding career, a higher income, better emotional well-being, and better health is easy once you release the negative emotions that prevent you from having these things. Once you learn the process, you can use it at any time and any place.

- Improved relationships
- Reduced stress levels
- Freedom from depression, anxiety, fear, anger, and other emotional challenges
- More energy
- Better health and a sense of vitality
- And much, much more

As stated previously, the Sedona Method helps you reach your goals by releasing any negative beliefs you may have that prevent you from attaining the things you want. It can also help you heal your past wounds to continue to drag your past's weight into your present. Negative episodes from your past can take your attention away from creating the life you desire, shackling you to situations in the past that make you feel resentment, regret, guilt, blame, and anger.

You will "let go" years of mental programs and stored thoughts in just a few seconds using the Sedona Method's special techniques. When you get an unwelcome emotion or a sense of resistance, you expel it. With a minimal feeling out of the way, you're free to build whatever outcome you want, anytime you want.

One way to use the Sedona approach is to help you accomplish your financial goals, such as wealth formation. People who want to gain wealth also set well-defined financial targets and then take the required steps to attain those goals. But soon, in their efforts, they sabotage themselves through the values they carry in their subconscious.

Suppose you set the goal of being wealthy while retaining the illusion that you do not deserve wealth, or that you are not clever enough to be rich, or that creating wealth involves making tremendous sacrifices. In that case, you will not allow yourself to be rich. It's like trying to grow a garden filled with weeds or keeping a plant safe when infested with pests.

And how does the Sedona Method help you develop wealth? After evaluating your financial targets, you should use the Sedona Method to address any hesitancy or reluctance that could arise from your value system against those goals. This opposition could be in the form of unease, confusion, suspicion, or anger. Any emotion that isn't optimistic or inspiring is a form of resistance. Releasing false values and feelings that stand in your way helps you see how you generate riches and bring abundance to your life.

Once you've released your negative beliefs and feelings about money and your worthiness to attract money, you'll be starting with a clean slate on which you can write anything you want. Go ahead and envision a life filled with all the wealth you can imagine and move forward toward the creation of that life without negative mental programming and feelings holding you back.

Dealing with negative emotions to raise your self-esteem

People with high self-esteem are not always happy. The difference between a person with high self-esteem and low self-esteem in terms of emotions is how they deal with their negative emotions.

You cannot prevent negative emotions from coming from time-to-time. Negative emotions are not "negative." They come to you to help you notice some unfulfilled need, or warn you of something in your life that needs to be changed. These emotions help you to build a balanced, healthy, and happy life. All uncomfortable emotions should therefore be listened to rather than ignored.

Many people with low self-esteem try to ignore their negative emotions. They may have learned through their childhoods that negative emotions are bad and should not be expressed, or they may not know how to handle their emotions. People with low self-esteem often translate having negative emotions into being a bad person. They assume that they are either doing something wrong or do not deserve to feel differently if they feel sad, angry, or scared.

People with high self-esteem listen to their emotions without ignoring them. They do not equate feeling bad with being bad. People with high self-esteem learn from their negative emotions and take active steps to make themselves feel better (for example, making sure they get their unfulfilled needs met).

To keep your self-esteem high, you thus have to accept your emotions. Ask yourself what you need to heal your wound or to find a better balance. If you need social support, ask for it! If you need to slow down and relax, do it! You may need to have a good cry to offload some pressure, and everything will be fine again. Welcome your emotions and listen to what they are trying to tell you!

Mending your thought process for peace

Anger can be a powerful motivator and can lead to great things if you can remain in control of it and utilize it to take assertive action toward positive outcomes that are not harmful to others. However, anger is a passionate emotion and can be a difficult beast to tame. If left untamed, it can control the way that you think. If you are unprepared for your anger, it can easily get the better of you and drive you toward actions that may be detrimental to your well-being and the well-being of others.

You must always remember that *you* are in control of your actions, not your anger. While you can't control the turbulence of life, nor can you control how you feel about certain situations, there are some things that you do have control over. You can control your awareness of your own anger and its effect on the people around you. You can control the way that you react to your anger. You can control how you communicate your anger. With practice, you can even control how you think about situations that may lead to anger.

There is a correlation between thought and emotion. The two processes occur in the brain and are closely linked to each other. One affects the other. A certain thought can spark an emotion in you, or indeed several emotions. The thought of approaching retirement may make you feel excited at the prospect of having more free time. Still, it may also make you feel nostalgic for years gone by and nervous about entering the next phase of your life. At the same time, different emotions can cause different thoughts to go through your mind. The excitement you feel about getting more free time may lead you to think about what you can do with that free time. The feeling of nostalgia may make you recall all the good times you've had with your co-workers and company. The feeling of nervousness may make you think uncertain thoughts, such as whether your finances can sustain retirement or whether you are emotionally ready to retire.

Just as anger can lead to angry thoughts, angry thoughts can lead to anger. Often, people who have a problem with anger don't even notice their angry thoughts. Angry thoughts become an automatic way of thinking. It creates a cycle of anger that will make you feel worse and worse as recurring angry thoughts flash into your mind over and over.

It is possible to break this cycle by taking a close look at your angry thoughts and analyzing a situation more objectively to see if you are interpreting it correctly. Angry people are more prone to taking things personally and seeking conflict that may not actually be there. Have you ever had an angry conversation with someone in a public place and spotted some of the people around you looking your way? You might see them looking and think to yourself, "Why are they staring at me?" or "These people should mind their own business," or "They're staring at me because they think I'm a jerk." However, how accurate are these thoughts? When thinking about the situation from an objective viewpoint, rather than from a place of anger, it's probably more likely that those people were simply glancing over in response to the raised volume of your voice. They probably couldn't care less about your conversation, and went straight back to their day once they saw what the source of the sound was.

When you are angry, you automatically expect negativity from other people, and you tend to see hostility where there is none to be found. To manage your anger, it is important to recognize and challenge these thoughts.

In the mid-1950s, psychologist Albert Ellis developed a technique called cognitive restructuring. This technique can control and change negative thoughts by reframing the situation that has triggered them. Since its development, cognitive restructuring has been used successfully to treat a wide variety of conditions, including depression, post-traumatic stress disorder, anxiety, social phobias, relationship issues, addictions, and stress.

This chapter will teach you how to use cognitive restructuring to analyze and reframe your angry thoughts. With practice, this is a technique that you will be able to use regularly, not just to address angry thoughts, but all types of negative thoughts.

Try to calm yourself

Suppose you are still feeling angry from the situation you have experienced. In that case, you will have a hard time effectively utilizing cognitive restructuring; therefore, the first step in the process is to calm yourself. Go to your calm-down kit if you need to. In fact, you can keep your calm-down kit next to the notepad you use for cognitive reframing.

Once you have successfully calmed yourself and reached a state of mind where you can be rational and objective, proceed to the next step.

Learn to identify the situation

Think about the situation that made you angry. For now, just think about it in terms of cold, hard facts. Describe for yourself the event or series of events as they happened.

To clearly outline the process of cognitive restructuring, let's refer to the example below. "The person I saw romantically broke up with me via text message."

This clearly defines the situation that has caused your anger in basic terms, without talking about emotion just yet.

Learn to analyze your mood

Next, write down the emotions you felt during this situation. Try to get down the entire range of emotions you felt, not just anger. Be sure to stick to just the emotions felt, not the thoughts associated with these emotions. For example, "I deserved more than just a text message" would be a thought. In contrast, the emotions associated with the thought would be anger, frustration, insecurity, and humiliation.

Once you have identified all the emotions you felt, write down what specifically about the situation made you angry. Was it the fact that the person broke up with you? Was it the fact that they didn't take the time to meet with you in person? Was it both? Whatever it was that made you angry, write it down. Even if the reason for your anger seems petty when you're looking at it on paper, be honest with yourself and leave nothing out.

Learn to identify your automatic thoughts

Next, identify and write down the thoughts that automatically went through your mind immediately after the event. These thoughts will most likely be negative and will be based upon your negative views of yourself and the world around you. If you are an angry person, your automatic thoughts will be motivated by emotions associated with anger, specific to the type of anger you exhibit. For example, suppose you are prone to a self-abusive style of anger. In that case, your automatic thoughts will be self-abusive in nature.

Typical types of automatic response include:

- Self-evaluated thoughts, ie. "I'm not worth a face-to-face breakup."

- Thoughts about the evaluation of others, ie. "They were always too good for me."
- Evaluative thoughts about other people, ie. "They must be seeing someone else."
- Thoughts about coping strategies, ie. "I really need a drink."
- Thoughts of avoidance, ie. "I just want to be alone."

You may have more automatic thoughts than this, so examine your thoughts carefully to ensure that you haven't missed any.

Figure out the supportive evidence

Now that you had written down the automatic thoughts that went through your mind when you experienced the triggering situation, identify and write down evidence that objectively supports your automatic thoughts. Cognitive restructuring aims to be honest with yourself and look at the situation from both sides. This means acknowledging your angry thoughts and trying to see if they are justifiable.

Here are some examples of supportive evidence for the previous automatic thoughts:

- "We hadn't seen each other for very long."
- "They were a very accomplished and attractive person."

- "We had been spending less and less time together lately."

Figure out the contradictive evidence

Next, examine your automatic thoughts from the other side of the scale. Identify and write down evidence that is contradictory to your automatic thoughts.

Here are some examples of contradictory evidence:

- "The time that we spent together had been enjoyable."
- "I am an accomplished person with many friends that care about me."
- "My partner was always honest in their interactions with me."
- "We had a lot in common."

Here, we can see that these statements tend to be fairer and more rational than automatic thoughts. They are less focused on negativity and generally consider the situation on a wider scale, taking an open view instead of the narrow view that comes from looking at things from a place of negativity.

Learn to identify the balanced thoughts

Now that you've looked at both sides of the situation, you are better equipped to take a fair and balanced view of the situation. Consider both the supportive evidence and the contradictory evidence and decide which evidence is more valid. You may combine two pieces of information to form more accurate statements than either individual side. Write down these statements, read them back to yourself, and really think hard about each statement. Decide whether each statement is balanced and rewrite them if you need to. If you are unsure whether you are managing a successful balance, try discussing your friends' situation to see what they think.

Once you have arrived at a balanced view, write down your balanced thoughts. For example:

- "While our relationship was enjoyable at times, our recent interactions had not been as fun."
- "We are both interesting people, but our personalities didn't match."
- "The way they ended the relationship was inappropriate, but also out of character. It might have been a result of things going on in their life that I don't know about."

Keep your mood in check

Now that you have a clearer view of the situation, write down how you are feeling now. Your feelings toward the situation will likely have improved from before you started this exercise. You are feeling less angry. The time that has been taken to re-evaluate the situation and the process both act in delaying your anger, refocusing your mind, and presenting a more objective perspective on the situation's events.

Now that you are in a calmer state, think about what you should do next. It's possible that after looking objectively at the situation, you have decided to pursue no further action. You may decide that the breakup was for the best and that the person probably had a good reason for ending it with a text. You may decide to move on and leave the door open if they wish to communicate with you more effectively in the future.

If you wish to take further action, you will be in a better state of mind to think of a course of action that will lead to a positive outcome. Rather than calling them up and leaving a tirade of angry voicemail messages, you choose to send them a polite text that tells them that you understand but feel hurt by the way they ended it. You may ask them if it would be okay to meet in person so that you can discuss the matter further.

However you choose to respond to the situation, by performing cognitive restructuring, you can guarantee that the action you choose to take will be rational and well thought out, rather than an automatic, potentially destructive response.

Learn to let go of destructive habits

First of all, you need to be aware that what you are doing is a negative thing and may have unfortunate implications in the future if you don't do something about it.

Many people don't change destructive habits because they don't know how. To start, you need to be aware of your destructive habits and desire to make a change. With time and effort, you can now stop habits that harm you, your life, and anything else around you. We have all read stories and seen movies about people that end up hitting rock bottom or have faced incredible challenges due to bad habits and have come out of this with their lessons learned and motivation to change their lives. Although this does happen, unfortunately, it's not as easy as the movies would lead you to believe.

Be aware that your journey is not going to be easy. It is not like in any of the movies you've seen or stories you've read. If you want to make it, you need to be mentally prepared to face whatever may come your way. You will even have to fight your being because it is not that easy to put an end to a habit that controls your life.

As you may know already, some habits are painful, and it isn't enough to feel bad about them to make them go away. And change won't occur after being kicked in the hind or trip and have a revelation. Change occurs gradually, and it is not as uplifting as many people would expect it to be; only after an extended period will we be able to see the real effects of our work.

So yes, it will be hard work at first, but it will be worth it because it will make your life much better than before. Even if there will be moments when you will feel like quitting, do have in mind that you are making all the effort for your well-being, happiness, and a better tomorrow.

Why is it so hard to change habits?

Well, our brain loves them because they are energy savers. Let us look at one simple example to understand what this means. For instance, when walking across your room at home and feel the need to sit down, you do this automatically, without thinking about it, because your brain assumes where the chair is. But you can't do the same in a new environment, like the room of a hotel, where you'll have to look for a chair. Thus, we say that traveling experiences are tiring because the brain has to readjust to the new environment.

According to researchers, habits are conditioned responses produced by our brain in a matter of milliseconds. It means that they are several thousand times quicker than any other conscious decision we make. Believe it or not, most of our decisions are also governed by our habits because the brain reacts to them faster and influences our decisional process. Our habits manifest more with ease when we are in familiar environments; this is why it is so difficult to control them.

You see, habits are like running on autopilot, while conscious decisions are like a manual override. Because we mostly function on autopilot, habits are taking place with priority. It happens when we are tired and lack our focus as well because we need attention and concentration to maneuver the manual override, in this case, to make conscious decisions.

Obviously, the autopilot is inexhaustible and never gets tired; fighting with habits is an ugly battle. So even if you know what you have to do to make things right, the conscious control may come too late after the habit already manifested.

Understanding why it is so difficult to keep habits in control will help you treat this matter with an adequate level of attention and commitment. You should not think that it is impossible to change or stop a habit because it is possible to better understand the process. The way a habit is introduced into your mind, it will be possible to take it out.

So, exactly when did a thought become a habit?

Through learning and repetitive behavior. So if you want to stop and change a habit, you will have to go through the same processes. The first step may be the opposite of what you might think. Do not try to understand your habit and what triggers it, but focus on becoming a person. Focusing on certain thoughts, feelings, and states, regardless if they are positive or negative, will only amplify them and make them of greater importance to your brain. This is why you have to change your focus on the things you want to obtain.

How would you like to feel? How would you like to be? How would you like to behave? Find answers to these questions and other questions that will help you design a new and improved version of yourself and focus on them.

You should also not think about the things you don't want to do. You may think that this should offer you more control, but it won't, and you'll end up doing exactly what you don't want to do. It is said that where attention goes, behavior follows. So if your attention slides to the things you don't want to do, there are high chances that the way you'll act will take you there.

The example of Adam and Eve and the forbidden fruit is a very plastic one of what we are talking about here. Even if they were told, repeatedly, not to eat it, they ended up doing what they weren't supposed to do. Instead of thinking about what you shouldn't do, you should focus on what you should do.

It is easier to develop new actions that contradict the bad habits than to completely remove the bad habits. You will have to learn to think about what you want to bring into your life, contrary to the old bad habits you want to remove.

Later on, we will talk about making a positive and desired action become a habit, changing your lifestyle into a desirable and happy one.

Once you know what you want to become and focus on the actions that will improve your life and who you are, do know that practice makes it better. It is not enough to find the positive replacement of your bad habits because you need to constantly practice and reinforce them if you want them to take over.

So, whatever you do, stop focusing on the negative aspects and the bad habits that you have, and drive all your attention to the person you want to become and the actions that will get you there.

How should I get rid of my bad habits then?

As mentioned previously, focusing your attention on the things you want to do, rather than on the things you don't want to do anymore, is a better strategy. So, the best way to get rid of a bad habit is by creating a brand new one.

Create a better version of the habit you want to change, a version that will bring you benefits and not disadvantages, which will make you better in the end. It is much easier to replace a habit than to try to erase it completely. Your mind will act like it knows the habit was there. It can be quite a challenge when trying to ditch an old habit because you will continuously think about it and be very hard to control.

So, why not use your energy and focus on developing a habit that could help you and make your life better. It can be any habit, anything you think that you would feel a positive change in your life once learned.

Of course, it sounds easier said than done, but if you are determined to make a change, nothing will stop you from making this happen. There's no point in saying that it's a piece of cake to create and learn a new habit because we need to be realistic. But no-one says that it is impossible either.

If you have a strong desire and a "must-have" attitude for a change to happen in your life, you will be to make it happen. In fact, if you are unhappy with the life you have or if you would like to correct some things about yourself, changing your habits is the best way to go.

We become the sum of our habits, some useful and positive. In contrast, others are not that useful, being bad and damaging. So, just making the right changes in your habits can help you become the person you want to be, who has the life you want to live.

Do you know what habits you would like to add? It is enough to think about the aspects you would like to improve about yourself and your life, and you will find the answer. If you are looking to create a new habit, you will have to know what habit it is, so you'll know how to work on it.

Some habits are easier to learn than others. Developing a habit of drinking a glass of water every morning upon waking may be pretty simple. Getting up every morning at 5 a.m. to go jogging may not be quite as simple. A harder goal will take more planning, patience, and a determination to succeed.

There isn't a set number of days to learn a habit. Old research suggests it takes 21 days to establish a habit. Researchers have since discovered that this is false. If someone tells you that they know a method of learning a new habit in "x" days, it is untrue because no-one can tell how many days are needed for your mind to develop a new habit.

The amount of time to develop a habit depends on the habit's complexity, familiarity with the habit, and the amount of repetition it receives. For a baby to develop the habit of walking when it has never walked a day, his life takes time and patience. But with "baby steps," he will eventually get there, which is the same for you.

With a bit of organization, practice, and patience, you will develop a new habit. Developing a new habit requires repetition. The more repetition, the faster your new behavior will become a habit.

The hardest habits to create are the habits that do not provide an immediate reward. Easier habits, the habit of accepting chocolate when someone offers it to you, are triggered by the reward of having chocolate (chocolate stimulates serotonin and dopamine, the happy chemicals of the body) almost immediately. When you sit down on the couch, you automatically turn on the TV, and you are rewarded with entertainment. So, what can you do when the habit you want to create is not giving you an immediate reward? First, start with very small habits, the tiny steps of the habit you want to accomplish in the end.

What are tiny habits?

It is a habit you will do at least once a day, which will not take you more than 30 seconds to do; it requires very little effort on your part. It is relevant for developing the desired behavior, so it will be like taking baby steps towards your goal. If you don't make your habits this small, the chances for you to change your behavior by adopting new habits are very slight.

It is best to start small than not starting at all. So, if you plan on jogging each morning, running for an hour won't help you. Most certainly, you will not go jogging the next day at all unless you have an iron will. But, if you start putting on your running shoes every day, even if you don't end up using them, it is a start. The idea is to make the task as easy as possible, so your mind won't be able to say no to it.

Once you are used to your tiny habit, it is time to expand it by moving to the next level. Don't be afraid to do so because it will seem easy, even if the habit is larger now. You already know a part of it, so it won't be that difficult. The more you practice something, the easier it becomes, so keep this in mind each time you consider your small habit difficult, hard, or complicated. It may look like this way now because you are not used to it but, as you continue practicing it, it will become easier with each passing day.

What makes a habit easier?

They seem easy because you do them every day. It doesn't feel like a thought-action anymore, being more an automated reaction after so much practice. All your habits will become this way if you keep practicing.

The next step involves performing this tiny habit right after a behavior or habit that already exists. This way, it will be easier for you to associate a habit that you are accustomed to and a new one you are introducing. It is easier to perform a tiny habit if you associate it with an existing one. For instance, if you want to start a habit of flossing your teeth, you should do it right after brushing the teeth. Here, the teeth brushing habit is an existing habit which you already do without difficulty every day. Because teeth flossing is a similar habit, it is easier to accomplish when associating it with teeth brushing.

Think about what habit you already have that could be associated with the new habit you want to introduce. Once you identify the existing habit, all you need to do is perform that tiny new habit right after performing the already embedded habit in your behavior.

Did you practice your new habit?

Well, this means you have reasons to celebrate. Yes, even a small victory like this one should count a lot and should be celebrated accordingly. In fact, you should not skip this part because reinforcing yourself for the good behavior you just had is the best way to shorten the period for learning a new habit. Your mind will be thrilled with the victory. It will be easier to remember that you have to do a certain habit, making it a permanent habit in a shorter amount of time. Experiencing positive emotions and feelings when you remember that you need to perform your tiny habit is another way to make the process shorter and faster. So, when starting a new habit, it is best to perform it a few times, each time feeling that you accomplished a great victory. This method will help your brain remember it and perform it easier.

Praising yourself and feeling good about doing something will help you with the task of making a tiny habit turn into a permanent habit. Remember to make this tiny habit after an existing habit and celebrate immediately afterwards. It doesn't matter how you celebrate or praise yourself, as long as you do it and it makes you feel good about it. In time, once you get the hang of this tiny habit, you will be able to expand it and reach the desired behavior by performing more complex habits. Practicing always makes it perfect, even in the case of habits.

Allowing Yourself to Grow Through Anger Management

If someone that you know came up to you and started suggesting you needed to get some anger management, you probably would not react too kindly to that. This is because it often implies that something is wrong with you. There are many stigmas associated with anger, management, and disengagement. Most people do not want to admit that they have a problem.

Anger management is a good thing. It is designed to help people, and it is not meant to stigmatize them. These programs are there to help you and others better control your anger in a way that won't cause harm to yourself or to others. They can also help you to find more opportunities for personal growth and development.

You may be curious as to how anger management will help you reach your full potential. This can happen by the following means:

It will help you to figure out what makes you angry

No matter what you may think about it, these anger episodes do not just appear out of nowhere. There is something, whether it is legitimate or not, that is causing that outburst. Being able to recognize what reason in particular that makes you angry is very important because then you can look out for some of the signs and avoid them later on.

If you can figure out what makes you feel unhappy and make you angry, you can learn how to make the appropriate changes to respond in the right manner. You will then be able to start working towards fixing these issues. Over time, this will help reduce how many times these outbursts occur.

Will allow you to deal with anger-related emotions

There are actually quite a few emotions that can come with the anger that you feel. These can include some emotions such as impulsiveness and aggression. These emotions are even worse because they can cause a lot of damage and make it more likely that these sudden anger episodes will increase. During anger management sessions, you will work not only on the anger you are feeling, but also on the other emotions tied to it.

When you take care of the anger and the other emotions that come with it, you improve your chances of keeping that rage under control. You are also working to reduce some of the damage that can come when you lose control with anger.

Teach you to manage your stress

One important thing that you will learn how to do when you work with anger management is how to manage your triggers. You will find that each person who is dealing with anger will have their own personal triggers. Part of learning how to manage anger is to learn how to react to your triggers to not react with anger.

This process will involve several steps, and it will work to modify the way you respond to stressful situations. Fixing how you think and react to the things that make you angry will help keep the anger episodes in control.

Mental Exercises to Keep Yourself Calm

Despite the best efforts that you are putting forth to deal with the triggers that are causing your bursts of anger, and the behavior patterns that come from it, there are some other and more holistic approaches that can help you make sure that you cover your bases and get that anger under control.

Many things will occur in your life, and you really do not have that much control over what happens and when it happens. However, you can control how you will respond to these situations. For some people, anger is a ticking time bomb that is always ready to go, but there are things that you can do yourself to defuse that ticking time bomb and keep that anger at bay.

No matter how badly you are feeling or how much you want to let anger get the best of you, there are always things that you can do to appropriately deal with the anger in your life. This chapter will focus on the techniques you can consider using to properly deal with your anger, regardless of what situations are going on around you.

Try some relaxation techniques

Any time you find yourself having to deal with your anger, try taking a step back to relax, and you will find that it's very beneficial. Relaxation techniques can help you control your anger bursts and relieve anxiety and stress, which may cause some of that anger. These techniques are also good at creating a feeling of wellness in the body too.

There are many different relaxation techniques that you can choose from, so go ahead and pick the one that works best for you. Breathing exercises, yoga, meditation, reading a good book, going on a walk, a hot bubble bath, and more are just some of the ideas you can use to help keep your anger under control. Anything that can help keep your mind away from angry, destructive thoughts and situations and help your body stay calm will work here.

Mindfulness

This is along the same lines, but mindfulness is all about an awareness of the present in terms of the circumstance and the moment. This concept comes from Buddhism, but it can still be used in our modern world. It is an effective anger management technique. It can be used to prevent many outbursts from happening in the future. This is because mindfulness is potent in calming down your thoughts to leave your problems behind. If you have never practiced mindfulness in the past, you will be happy to know that the process is pretty simple. The first step is to start paying attention to all the things that are going on around you, such as the sounds, smells, sights, and distractions. Second, you will then need to put all your attention on one element of the existing moment, such as your breathing, so that you can meditate and immerse yourself into a peaceful trance. The most important part is that if you have trouble meditating, all you have to do is to focus your energy on the present moment. There are many good resources that you can use to help you out with practicing the technique of mindfulness if you find that it's too difficult for you. Those who concentrate on their anger too much may find that focusing on the present moment, or on anything other than their anger, can be difficult. But with some practice and some help along the way, you will get it down to enjoy all the benefits it can offer.

Learn to breathe

If you are angry and feel that you are losing your control a little bit, it is good to learn how to breathe to take a step back from the situation. Take slow and steady breaths in and out. Most people find that counting to ten or to twenty while they are breathing helps them to take a long enough timeout that they will feel better. Plus, when you are counting, you can focus on something other than your anger, which can help make it go away much faster.

Use visualization

This often works well with some of the other techniques, but you can do it on your own if you want to. Visualization is not about fantasizing about how you would take out your rage on someone who is (or who you think is) causing all your rage. Rather, it is more about helping you find different ways to cool off before your anger starts to take over again. While the first situation may seem like it would satisfy you, it is probably something you have done at some point; it is really not the best way for you to calm down.

A better thing to do is to imagine a bath that is full of hot water. This water is boiling, steaming, and hard to even touch. Then you need to see yourself physically cooling that water until it is nice and warm, without being too hot. This will help your mind have something new to focus on other than your anger, and it will give you time to cool down a little bit.

Chapter 16: The Minimalistic Life - Baby Steps to Buddhism

Buddhism encourages an individual to pursue a life where you only have the absolute minimum that you need to survive but, in our day and age, simplifying our lives to that extreme might seem a bit difficult.

Suppose you don't want to completely eliminate everything in your life and yet want to follow Buddhism's footsteps. In that case, the following ideas might help you take the first baby steps to start your journey. Once you have adjusted yourself to these subtle changes, you can slowly move forward to the more extreme ones.

There are different ways of defining a simple life. What a simple life is to you can mean a totally different thing to another person. However, the best way of defining a simple life is by understanding that it centers around the idea of getting rid of what you deem unessential in your life. In other words, it means spending most of your time doing what you value the most. A simple life means avoiding wasting your valuable time on things that are not important. As such, you value-create time for people and experiences that add meaning to your life. About clutter, it means freeing your mind from potential distractions that could prevent you from thinking straight and enjoying life.

Living a simple life is not as simple as it sounds. It's something that calls for patience simply because it's a journey and not a destination. The easiest way to understand how to live a simple life is by identifying the things that are important to you and eliminating everything else. However, to ensure that you understand this in detail, the following are practical tips to bear in mind when looking to simplify your life:

List down the important things

Start by identifying what you value most in your life. Make a list of these things. While doing this, you must limit this list to 4 or 5 items. The importance of limiting your list to a few things is that it creates room for important things in your life that may arise later. As a result, attending to the first will create a more fulfilling feeling than randomly approaching life.

Evaluate your time usage

It is also crucial that you evaluate how you spend your time. Monitor how you use your time from the time you wake up to the end of the day. Create a list of the things that you often prioritize and those that usually distract you. By doing this frequently, you will identify things that only consume time and are not important to you. In other words, you can redesign your day and work productively towards achieving your daily goals.

Learn to say no

A fundamental habit that you ought to develop as you try to simplify your life is to learn to say no. Indeed, it is never easy to say no to your friends and colleagues at work. Unfortunately, this creates a situation where your to-do list will always be packed. You should understand that other people will be completing their tasks because you help them do what needs to be done on their to-do lists. On your end, you will have a lot pending. This is because you chose to accept extra tasks without putting yourself first; therefore, it's never bad to say no when you are doing it for the right reasons.

Cut down your media consumption

With technological advancements, you can now access details at the click of a button. This makes it easier for us to connect with our loved ones and mates on the plus side. People's and companies' communication methods have shifted as a result of social media. People should realize that excessive media consumption can be harmful. It pollutes our minds by altering our pre-existing views of life. Based on our newly-formed views, we end up creating new ways of living our lives. Unfortunately, this is how we make our lives more difficult.

Declutter your physical space

Simplifying your life necessitates decluttering your physical room. When compared to a cluttered workspace, it is easier to work in a tidy environment. Clutter makes it difficult to think clearly. Begin by decluttering the room around you before tackling the clutter in your head, as previously suggested. Get rid of something in your home that doesn't add value to your life. Much of the time, we hang on to things without understanding that they are just taking up space for more important things. You should work on decluttering your space, from your bedroom to your kitchen. In an ideal world, the physical environment you build would also positively affect how you think and make decisions.

Spend time doing what you love

When you get rid of the things that aren't important in your life, you'll have more time to reflect on the things that are. As a result, make the most of this time by doing something you enjoy. Remember the important stuff list you made? Use this extra time to get this stuff done. You will eventually live a simple but satisfying life.

Get rid of toxic people

It will be daunting to live a simple life when you're surrounded by toxic people. These are people who never seem to add value to your life in any way. The worst thing is that they drain energy from you as they always think negatively. Also, they are the people that push you around to help them without stopping to help you. Sure, some of these individuals are your best friends because there is a lot that you have been through with them. However, a keen eye on your relationship with them will reveal nothing you benefit from being friends with them. So, the best thing you can and should do is to eliminate them from your life. This might sound harsh, but, the reality is that you will be doing yourself a favor by opening doors for more fruitful relationships.

Plan your meals wisely

Living a simple life also means that you should plan what you eat. Eating is part of your daily routine.

This is something that you do throughout the day as long as you feel hungry. Accordingly, planning for your meals shouldn't be neglected. Make it a priority on your to-do list. Don't waste your time every day trying to figure out what you will be having for lunch or dinner. Just plan it. The good news is that doing this increases the likelihood of eating healthy foods that contribute to a productive lifestyle.

Address your debts

Often, people choose to ignore the debts that they have with the hopes that it will help them stop worrying. This doesn't help since you will only procrastinate the decision to pay your debts. Come up with a plan of how you will pay off your debts. Financially, it will help you make better decisions and open doors for business opportunities.

A simple life doesn't have to be something that is beyond your reach. It's all about identifying the things that are of great importance to you and prioritizing them. This creates time for you to enjoy yourself with family and friends, so live a simple life by keeping in mind the tips discussed in this chapter.

Chapter 17: The Different Rituals of Buddhism to Know About

Buddhism, having been around for so long, is saturated in traditions and rituals. A ritual can be as simple as meditation or as elaborate as the Buddha statue's ceremonial blessing. You don't have to participate in these rituals just because you follow a Buddhist lifestyle, but if you wish to immerse yourself in the traditions fully, they are pertinent parts of the Buddhist way of life. Though some of these rituals will be explained below, it is not nearly the extent of how Buddhists pay homage to the Buddha and to their heritage. Suppose you are interested in learning the more sacred rituals. In that case, it is advised to contact your local temple and seek a teacher's guidance. As you take in this chapter's information, you will hear words such as blessings and reverence, but remember they are not connected to worship. Instead, most of Buddhism's traditions are there to show thanks to the Buddha for his teachings and his guidance. Just as you would thank a teacher in school, the Buddhists find that paying homage to Buddha for his lessons is pertinent since they will lead to the end of their suffering in the cycle of life. You may choose to participate in these or just silently and personally give thanks for the Buddha's teachings. Here are some of the rituals practiced in Buddhism:

Bowing Down to Show Respect

Bowing is a simple tradition, also known as prostration, and is done each time that you approach a likeness of the Buddha in a place of meditation or teaching. Each person is supposed to prostrate three times by kneeling on a stool in front of the Buddha with both of your palms facing up. During the first bow, turning one hand represents the cultivation of wisdom inside you, while the other represents the offering of compassion to others. Therefore, your open palms mean wisdom and compassion. You may also bow when you are done with yoga or meditation sessions if it seems correct in that situation. Giving thanks to the Buddha will not be frowned upon. It may even light that spark of hope within your heart that your meditation will be fruitful and that you will learn the ways of Buddha with the respect that these lessons should be approached with.

The Different Chants

You may be familiar with the rhythmic sounds of monks chanting in the temples. Chanting is more than just singing. It is the representation and reminder to live a life of discipline, perseverance, and charity. These things are brought to light through chanting which is the repetitious singing of Buddha's teachings. The sound itself can be soothing and close to the universal sound of connectivity to the earth, or Ohm, as the Buddhist practice refers to it. However, there is no particular pitch or tone required for chanting. These chants can be done at any time during a ceremony or before and after meditation. Often when meditating with a teacher, they will chant during your meditation as a way to remember the Buddha's teachings and bring the true self closer to the realization of enlightenment.

Importance Of Gongs

These instruments are used for several different things. In the ceremony, gongs and singing bowls signal the beginning or end of a teaching or event. During meditation, they are used to begin meditation by creating a universal tone to focus. They are also used to end the meditation and bring the practitioner carefully from their rested state.

Gongs are also specifically used during chanting to aid in focus, tone, and remembrance. Many people choose to have these types of instruments in their personal meditation space, though usually on a much smaller scale than what can be found in a temple. However, they are useful to remind practitioners of the seriousness of meditation, start the session with a traditional opening, and close the session.

Incense Lighting

Incense is not just used as a fragrant appliance during meditation; it is also used in rituals. The incense lighting is a reminder that you break free from the cycle of life, suffering, death, and rebirth. It is an homage you pay to the original true teacher as he guides you on your path to freedom through his teachings. The lit incense also plays a focal point during meditation to help guide you into a deeper state of stillness.

Buddhists also use lit incense as an offering to the Buddha in exchange for his blessing on their path. Though Buddha is not seen as a Christian God, some worship him as their leader in the enlightenment path. How you personally choose to use the tool is entirely personal and up to you and your beliefs.

Altar Offerings

If you visit a temple, you will often find offerings laid on a table for the Buddha in thanks. These offerings are usually fruit, flowers, or sometimes vegetarian dishes. The Chinese New Year is a time of great offerings, giving thanks to the Buddha for his guidance through the last year. You can create offerings of your own in your home meditation space. When the offerings begin to wilt or decay, you can simply remove them and discard them in the manner in which you feel most comfortable. Offerings also don't have to be listed above as some use branches, rocks, and other natural finds as offerings in a showing of connectivity with the world around you. If you care to create your own meditation area in your garden, choose a Buddha with a bowl, and as the different flowers come out in the garden, you can offer fresh flowers to the Buddha before you start your meditation and thus mix your enjoyment of nature with your enjoyment of sharing and learning to take your meditational practice seriously. When a flower wilts, then replace it with a fresh one and keep your altar alive, encouraging yourself to be reminded of your Buddhist ways.

Taking Shelter/Refuge

The Buddhist tradition of taking refuge does not mean that you shut yourself away, but instead that you immerse yourself completely in Buddhism. You take a vow of sorts to live the complete life of a Buddhist no matter what life may throw at you. The ceremony is deeply spiritual and connected to Buddhism and is performed by your teacher. At this level, it is necessary to have a teacher who can show you and teach you everything involved in giving yourself to Buddhism. This is not something to take lightly or do on a whim; it is a commitment. It said that the teachings and what you have learned of the understanding of the Buddhist path will travel with you to the next life when one takes refuge. You are not required to change your friends, faith, or anything of that nature, but you are vowing to live a life for others' positive forward progression.

The ceremony of taking refuge can be a bit long but thoroughly explains your duties as a Buddhist and offers the protection of Buddha himself. At the end of the ceremony, the different teachers or monks will drape a white or blue scarf over your shoulders as a sign of respect and protection. You will also receive a traditional Buddhist name different from your own, and it is assigned during this ritual.

Confessing Your Sins

Confession may be a familiar word to those who are familiar with the Christian religion or Catholics. However, it does not hold the same connotation in Buddhism. Confession is simply a way, through prayer, or speaking to a teacher or monk, to allow yourself to be released from guilt so that you may be able to see the truth behind the actions. Buddha cannot dissolve your transgression, but he does not scorn either. Karma is set in stone, a consequential chain of events that even the Buddha cannot disrupt. Therefore, the confession itself is used as a tool to teach you of the ego behind your actions, the outcome of negativity, and how to approach the same situation in the Buddhist way. You don't always have to talk to someone, which is where prayer comes into play. You release your guilt, suffering to the Buddha, and in return, begin to understand the truth behind your actions. It is important to remember Karma and how, for every good deed, you will find light and happiness, and for every bad one, Karma will reap its revenge. That in itself sounds terrifying, but we must remember an equal reaction to every action, there is a reaction to every action, sometimes good and sometimes bad depending on the action. This is the same for Karma. Confession does not clear you of this, but that is not what it is about; it is about learning and growing in self so that you will eventually reach that state of enlightenment. You may find that confession in your own space at home will help you make your life's journey more in keeping with the Nobel Eight Fold Path and study your own progress as you go through your meditation by keeping a journal of the confessions that are hindering your process. If you do not wish to write them down, saying them can help you reap the benefits of understanding and learning what you are doing in your life that may block your route towards enlightenment.

Precept Ceremony

The Precept Ceremony is almost always included in and associated with taking refuge. However, it is also often done at the end of other ceremonies. The person involved is relaying and taking oath in the five precepts which connect with the Three Truths. This ceremony is the most commonly performed ritual in Buddhism and shows the attendee's devotion to the Buddhist practice. The monk or teacher performing the ritual often covers their face with a fan that demonstrates the ceremony as general instead of personal. The relationship between the teacher and student has nothing to do with relaying the precepts and should be done by any person giving their vow and devotion to Buddhist ways. This ceremony, unlike others, must be done by a higher member of a Buddhist community or temple.

Dedication of Merit

The Dedication of Merit is one of Buddhism's very actions that shows the care and love of the world and living beings around us. It is the process of sharing all the good, all the teachings, and all the merit that one has collected with the world. The process involves thinking, or wishing, one singular, extraordinary outcome for the world and pushing that out in the universe using your collected positives as weight. This process is completely selfless and should be entered into with no self-serving thoughts at all. This creates a positive effect in the universe and teaches the person how to give with no selfish undertones. The Dedication of Merit can be done as a ceremony or simply through stillness and meditation internally.

However, it is important to understand that this dedication will not only fail to work but will also create a Karmic backlash in your direction if done with malice, negativity, or selfishness. During dedications, prayer and everyday acts should be done to create positivity in the world, not in your own life. Karma recognizes self-serving acts; you cannot fool the universe. This is part of the Enlighted path and shows how once you reach that heightened level, everything you do will come naturally as a selfless act.

Embracing The Art Of Meditation

The last ritual we will talk about has been spoken about throughout this book but has not been realized as an actual ritualistic act. Meditation is there to help you learn how to control your conscious mind, explore your true self, and connect the self with the body and the breath. Breathing is an exercise in meditation that cannot be left out. This does not mean that you can possibly meditate without breathing; this simply means that

You may have a challenging time understanding meditation as a ritual, but if you think about the base of a ritual, it is anything that is repeatedly done in reverence to something or someone else. Meditation is used as a tool to your path to enlightenment and should be done daily. Meditation is a sacred ritual in the Buddhist way of life and is done several times every day in temples and centers.

Rituals and traditions are longstanding inside of the Buddhist community. Many of these include prayer, devotion, and experience but if they are something that interests you, starting out with a Buddhist lifestyle is the first step. Monks and teachers have devoted their lives to furthering the path of enlightenment and the positive and peaceful spread of knowledge across the globe. Many of these rituals are performed daily, especially meditation, and to watch them can be truly life-changing. After you set up your home meditation space and study further into a life in the Buddhist practice, you will find that some do without even think about it. Each day bowing has become part of my routine and not out of habit but out of thankfulness for the teachings that the first Buddha laid out for the world.

The truth is hidden in all of the enlightenment, and is something that can be achieved through dedication and an open self. The calm and real life of a Buddhist lacks selfishness, adverse actions, and disrespect. Through empathy, love, and peace, the Buddha will guide you through the steps and lessons that you will need to take with you each day from the time you wake in the morning until you rest your head at night. These lessons will infiltrate past your conscious mind and go right to the heart of your true self, allowing for an opening in your life that will only be filled with real and unrepented kindness towards others. Remember, we are all creatures of the same earth, connected through a string that leads us from birth to death and back again.

Chapter 18: What to do Next?

Now that you know pretty much everything about the basics of Buddhism, what should you do next?

Well, Buddhism's effectiveness largely depends on how much you can incorporate it into your life and how deeply you can follow it.

Suppose this is your very first time taking a journey through The Noble Eightfold Path. In that case, there are certain steps that you can take that would allow you to pursue Buddhism further with greater devotion.

Take Regular Walks of Contemplation

Walking is one of the four postures taught by Buddha, and it is a form of meditation that helps us practice mindful awareness. In our daily lives, we can take frequent walks while appreciating the natural beauty that surrounds us. Take walks in various places. Mobile apps like AllTrails, which covers over 50,000 trails in Canada and the United States, make it simple to discover fresh and beautiful trails.

Participating in a walking retreat is another way to learn more about the Buddhist religion. These activities put a new twist on meditation retreats by encouraging us to practice mindfulness in groups while walking in beautiful locations.

Try to Make Friends With a Spiritual Side

Engaging in thoughtful conversation with other people is one of the best ways to explore our spirituality. It is now easier than ever to contact these people, thanks to advances in technology that enable us to communicate with those who share common interests.

There are over 1,300 meet-up groups for Buddhists all over the world. They range from meditation groups and book clubs to general hangouts, so you'll be able to communicate with those who have common interests and want to talk about their faith with others.

Explore Buddhist Musicians

Modern musicians are discovering new ways to communicate their Buddhist faith through music. Jen Shyu, a jazz guitarist, explains Buddhist ceremonies and lessons in her songs, while Kansho Tagai, also known as MC Happiness, is a monk/rapper who mixes Buddhist sutras with Hip-Hop. Both musicians use various musical styles to spread the Dharma, enabling Buddhists worldwide to communicate with their faith in new ways. Jen Shyu's music can be found on Deezer, Spotify, and YouTube.

Use Mindfulness Apps

We can practice mindfulness and meditation on the go, thanks to mobile technology. So, if you're having difficulty finding time to explore your religion, apps can be extremely helpful. Several smartphone applications allow us to practice meditation at times of the day when we are least likely to do so:

Buddhify 2 is an app that provides 11 hours of customized meditation plans for 15 different times of the day, such as work breaks and commutes. Some plans also target specific moods and situations, such as "stressed."

Equanimity is a meditation technique that helps us to monitor our sessions daily to form a habit.

We can record our sittings' time, date, and duration, and we can keep track of our emotional states in the notes section.

Daily Buddhist Prayers, which is also available for Android users, teaches new prayers in a transliteration format daily. Each prayer has an audio guide, as well as English translations and explanations.

Apart from that, you can also join your local yoga class or a place where you can practice meditation with fellow like-minded people.

And if you are really serious, you can consult with your local monastery and temporarily join them to explore your spiritual side.

Conclusion

My heart is filled with immense joy, thinking that you could read the book all the way through to the end.

I sincerely hope that you found the information within this manuscript easy to understand and valuable. Even if this book helped ease your anxiety or mental stress by a little bit, I would consider myself a success.

Before you leave, I would like to convey my heartiest gratitude to you for purchasing this book. Amazon is completely packed to the brim with similar books, and yet you gave my book a chance and checked it out.

I really appreciate it and thank you for it. Now, if it's not too much trouble, then I would **ask you to be kind enough to take just a moment of your time and leave a review for this book on Amazon.** It would immensely help me and encourage me to produce more high-quality content such as this in the future.

Your valuable feedback will let me know how I am doing and understand what kind of books my readers desire. And if you loved it, please let me know. Thank you, dear reader, for your valuable time and attention.

I wish you all the very best in your life and hope that the information that you learned from this book helps you find your lost love once more!

Copyright © 2021 Financementor

All rights reserved. No part of this publication may be reproduced, distributed, or transmitted in any form or by any means, including photocopying, recording, or other electronic or mechanical methods, without the prior written permission of the publisher, except in the case of brief quotations embodied in critical reviews and certain other noncommercial uses permitted by copyright law. Any references to historical events, real people, or real places can be real or used fictitiously to respect anonymity. Names, characters, and places can be products of the author's imagination.

Printed by Amazon.

Financementor
16 rue du Pont Neuf, 75001 Paris, France

Made in the USA
Columbia, SC
06 September 2021

FAILURE to FILE